THE CLOUGH WALK

© Martin Perry and Geoff Smith, 2016

All Rights Reserved. No part of this publication may be reproduced, stored in a retrieval system, or transmitted in any form or by any means – electronic, mechanical, photocopying, recording, or otherwise – without prior written permission from the publisher or a licence permitting restricted copying issued by the Copyright Licensing Agency, 90 Tottenham Court Road, London W1P 0LA. This book may not be lent, resold, hired out or otherwise disposed of by trade in any form of binding or cover other than that in which it is published, without the prior consent of the publisher.

Moral Rights: The authors have asserted their moral right to be identified as the Authors of this Work.

Published by Sigma Leisure – an imprint of Sigma Press, Stobart House, Pontyclerc, Penybanc Road, Ammanford, Carmarthenshire SA18 3HP.

British Library Cataloguing in Publication Data
A CIP record for this book is available from the British Library.

ISBN: 978-1-910758-07-6

Typesetting and Design by: Sigma Press, Ammanford.

Cover photographs: clockwise from top left: Trent Bridge; Roker Beach; Brian Clough Statue at Old Market Square, Nottingham; Brian Clough Statue at Albert Park, Middlesbrough.

Photographs: © Martin Perry

Maps: Mapping data Licenced from Ordnance Survey © Crown Copyright 2016 Licence number GV-215554

Printed by: Akcent Media

Disclaimer: the information in this book is given in good faith and is believed to be correct at the time of publication. No responsibility is accepted by either the authors or publisher for errors or omissions, or for any loss or injury however caused. Only you can judge your own fitness, competence and experience. Do not rely solely on sketch maps for navigation: we strongly recommend the use of appropriate Ordnance Survey (or equivalent) maps.

THE CLOUGH WALK
from Nottingham to Sunderland

Martin Perry and Geoff Smith

PREFACE

When we first read about the Clough Walk the first thing that struck us all was how incredibly appropriate it is. Dad loved walking. He loved wildlife and nature and being out in the open air and his many strolls along beaches, in fields, up hills and the odd mountain gave him the freedom to enjoy these simple pleasures.

The Walk really does trace his personal and professional footsteps and subsequently the footsteps of our family – the trail passing through our birthplaces of Hartlepool and Sunderland is a moving reminder for us, his children, of our own wonderful heritage.

With the passing of our beautiful Mum, Barbara, in 2013 the Walk holds an even greater poignancy. She was always by Dad's side and the roller coaster of a journey from the North East to the Midlands was made very much together.

We would like to say a sincere thank you to Martin Perry and Geoff Smith for their dedication to the project and for spending five years planning this wonderful tribute to our Dad. He would be happy and humbled by the honour. We, of course, are very proud and hope that all those inspired to take part in The Clough Walk will enjoy the experience as much as Dad would have and as much as he would want others to.

Hope to see you along the way!

Simon, Nigel and Elizabeth Clough

To Chris (Martin's wife) for her patience and support over the five years it took to complete the walk. Also grateful thanks to David Ewing for the Dewsbury link.

CONTENTS

Introduction		9
Summary of the Walk		11
Accommodation		17
Brian Clough at Nottingham		19
Stage 1 Trent Bridge to Sawley	10.8 miles	20
Stage 2 Sawley to Derby	9.6 miles	24
Brian Clough at Derby		29
Stage 3 Derby to Belper	8.5 miles	31
Stage 4 Belper to Matlock	10.5 miles	35
Stage 5 Matlock to Baslow	9.2 miles	39
Stage 6 Baslow to Heatherdene	11 miles	43
Stage 7 Heatherdene to Langsett	12.5 miles	48
Stage 8 Langsett to Clayton West	8.5 miles	52
Stage 9 Clayton West to Batley	14.5 miles	57
Stage 10 Batley to Apperley Bridge	11.5 miles	64
Brian Clough at Leeds		69
Stage 11 Apperley Bridge to Harewood	12.3 miles	70
Stage 12 Harewood to Knaresborough	9.7 miles	75
Stage 13 Knaresborough to Boroughbridge	9.4 miles	80

Stage 14	Boroughbridge to Thirsk	11.5 miles	83
Stage 15	Thirsk to Brompton	12 miles	87
Stage 16	Brompton to Yarm	13 miles	91
Stage 17	Yarm to Middlesbrough	11.5 miles	95
Brian Clough at Middlesbrough			99
Stage 18	Middlesbrough to Hartlepool	10.3 miles	101
Brian Clough at Hartlepool			105
Stage 19	Hartlepool to Seaham	14 miles	106
Stage 20	Seaham to Roker Park	8 miles	114
Brian Clough at Sunderland			120

Mileage Charts	121
Maps and Guides	124
Tourist Information Centre Telephone Numbers	125

INTRODUCTION

Brian Clough was arguably one of the most charismatic and inspirational figures of the second half of the twentieth century. Even if you are not remotely interested in association football you've probably heard of him. If you are a football devotee then you will be well aware of his outstanding contribution to the game both as a player and a manager.

As a player he represented two north eastern clubs, Middlesbrough and Sunderland scoring an unbelievable 251 goals in 274 matches before injury ended his playing career at the age of 29. This proved somewhat fortuitous as he quickly developed an outstanding gift for coaching and became manager of a third north eastern club, Hartlepool United, at the age of 30. His work ethic and leadership brought hard earned success and led him to quite amazing achievements at Derby County and Nottingham Forest only interrupted by a brief acrimonious spell at Leeds United. It is for his achievements at Nottingham Forest that he is best remembered as they became English Champions in 1978 and then European Champions in 1979 and 1980.

The Clough Walk is many things. It is a long distance walk that offers all the delights of planning and realisation but it is never taxing or arduous. It can be challenging to a fit and dedicated walker over a short time scale or a delight to a more mature walker. There are sections of the walk that can stand alone. The walk from Derby to Leeds is a walk up the spine of the country and the section from Yarm to Sunderland is an opportunity to connect with the traditions and feel of the North East of England. It's also an opportunity to walk the entire length of Yorkshire from south to north.

There are other well known and well established 200 mile walks but the Clough Walk offers that wonderful sense of achievement but with the security of relatively easy walking throughout.

It is essentially a walk through a man's life. Admittedly it starts at the end and finishes in the north east where he began his life but there are reasons for this. First of all it always makes sense to walk from south to north because of prevailing winds and the fact that with sunlight at your back the way ahead is well lit for appreciation of views. Secondly there is a greater sense of finality and achievement when finishing on a beach by the sea.

The walk really identifies with Brian Clough the man. Walkers need organisation, application, determination and an intrinsic respect for what is around them. The photograph below shows myself standing next to Brian

Clough at the Wilford Meadows School Annual Award Ceremony in 1991. I wrote to him and asked him to be our guest of honour with little expectation as he was experiencing difficulties at Nottingham Forest at the time. To my delight he readily agreed. Unsurprisingly he arrived on time and was absolutely wonderful with the pupils in a very humble way as if the pleasure was all his.

Brian Clough achieved what he did through passion, determination and hard work. He turned setbacks, his injury and the acrimony at Leeds, into triumphs. He represented standards and could implement them. Who else could have insisted on 'no swearing' from the Nottingham Forest supporters and achieved a 100% positive response.

The Clough Walk is a beautiful and invigorating walk from the Midlands through Derbyshire, Yorkshire and Cleveland and finishing on the coast of the North East of England. It requires planning, dedication and enthusiasm and is a fitting testimony to an inspirational figure of our times.

Martin Perry

SUMMARY OF THE WALK

The Brian Clough Walk is a 200 mile walk mainly through beautiful countryside but incorporates the cities and towns associated with his illustrious career both as a player and a manager. It affords the walker the opportunity to visit the football grounds if they wish.

The start of the walk

The walk begins in Nottingham and starts from Trent Bridge. You follow the River Trent out of Nottingham and past the Attenborough Nature Reserve. A short distance further on is Sawley where you link up with the River Derwent and having walked through Draycott you begin a 50 mile acquaintance with the Derbyshire Heritage Trail.

As you walk into Derby you pass the current home of Derby County F.C., Pride Park, but there is an opportunity to make a brief detour to their original home, the Baseball Ground. You leave Derby via Darley Abbey village and walk through Little Eaton and the Chevin enjoying spectacular views down the Derwent valley on your way to Belper. You leave Belper via the beautiful weir and walk over hills to Ambergate where you join the Cromford Canal. This takes you through the Cromford tunnel and over an impressive aquaduct before arriving in Cromford.

Cromford Tunnel

A short walk takes you into the tourist resort of Matlock Bath with its famous cable car to the Heights of Abraham. You leave by ascending High Tor and then descend into Matlock. You leave Matlock with a riverside walk before crossing fields to Rowsley. Then comes one of the undoubted highlights as you pass through the grounds of Chatsworth House on your way to Baslow. From Baslow you follow the River Derwent through Froggat, Grindleford and Shatton to the Heatherdene car park adjacent to the impressive Lady Bower Resevoir.

Lady Bower Reservoir

The route then skirts the Lady Bower, Derwent and Howden reservoirs, passing two dams, before passing over Howden Moor to Langsett. After climbing out of Langsett you experience a classic balcony walk round Hartcliffe Hill before descending to Thurlston. You now continue past Scout Dyke reservoir and after a brief dalliance with the Peniston Boundary Walk you arrive in Lower Denby. You then cross Bagden Park to join the Kirklees Way and follow it into the quaint village of Clayton West.

The next few miles afford you the pleasure of entering Flockton via Elvis Presley Boulevard before walking through Pithill Plantation to the stunning Thornhill Edge. After crossing the Calder & Hebble Navigation Canal and the River Calder you circumnavigate Dewsbury and pass through the delightful Caulms Wood to arrive at Batley.

Next comes 24 miles of the Leeds Country Way. It is a surprisingly exhilarating walk taking in two golf courses, two cricket grounds, an airport, a country estate, a country park and the beautiful River Aire before leaving it at Emmerdale (yes, the television village) in the grounds of Harewood House.

The Calder and Hebble Navigation Canal

On leaving the Harewood Estate you enjoy the delights of a riverside path followed by a walk to Knaresborough across rolling countryside, taking in the lovely village of Spofforth along the way.

Knaresborough to Boroughbridge is a comfortable 9.4 mile walk but the more dedicated walker may wish to add on the 11.5 miles to Thirsk as it is all very flat and easy walking.

The easy walking continues as you make your way across fields and woodland from Thirsk to Northallerton followed by a short road walk to Brompton.

Brompton to Yarm is a delightful country lane walk of 13.5 miles that can be completed quickly in all weathers with little or no traffic. It incorporates Long Lane, Deighton Lane, Back Lane, Saltergill Lane and Allerton Balk Lane and passes through the beautiful village of Appleton Whiske at the mid-point of the walk.

From Yarm you follow the beautiful Teesdale Way, which follows the River Tees through the Quarry Wood Nature Reserve at Eaglescliffe, past the replica of the *HMS Bark Endeavour*, along the wonderful riverside at Stockton with its impressive range of bridges and finishes at the Middlesbrough Transporter Bridge and in sight of the Riverside Football Stadium.

Cowpen Bewley

Middlesbrough to Hartlepool is a surprising delight, visiting the lovely village of Cowpen Bewley before using the Three Villages Native Tree Walk to arrive at Summer Hill Park and then entering Hartlepool via Burn Valley Park.

Leaving Hartlepool from the war memorial you pass the *HMS Trincomalee* and the Victoria Park Football Ground before arriving at the coast. You then enjoy a superb beach walk to Crimdon Dean.

From Crimdon Dean the route follows the Durham coastal path through Blackhall to Seaham Harbour and on to the River Wear. After crossing the river you follow a landscaped walk to Roker Pier and then on to the end of the walk at Roker Park.

"When our dad suffered the injury that ended his playing career prematurely he refused to accept it and spent many determined lonely hours running up and down the Cat and Dog steps at Roker Beach"- Simon Clough.

Before starting your walk you may wish to visit the Brian Clough statue (see front cover) which can be found in Nottingham just off Market Square at the bottom of King Street.

The end of the walk at Roker Beach

ACCOMMODATION

Accommodation is plentiful throughout most of the walk. Nottingham, Derby, Belper, Matlock and Baslow offer a range from hotel to B&B. At Heatherdene there is the famous Yorkshire Bridge Inn. Alternatively you can abort the day's walking by ½ a mile by going right off the old railway line, crossing stepping stones over the river and stay in Bamford. There are hotels and the Swallowholme campsite.

The only problem on the entire walk occurs at Langsett. On emerging onto the A616 the walker will need to turn left and walk one mile up the A616 to the Flouch Roundabout where there are regular bus services to Peniston and

Approaching Crimdon Dean

Holmfirth (famous for *The Last of the Summer wine*).The walk then continues from the A616 at Langsett to Clayton West where there is accommodation.

Arriving at Batley signals the start of two days walking on the Leeds Country Way. It is recommended that accommodation is obtained in Leeds (there is plenty right next to the bus station) and then bus transport is used to and from Batley, Apperley Bridge and Harewood.

The towns of Knaresborough, Boroughbridge, Thirsk, Northallerton (Brompton), Yarm, Middlesbrough, Hartlepool and Seaham offer numerous hotels and B&Bs.

At the end of the walk at Sunderland you can choose between staying in the city centre or in Roker or Seaburn overlooking the sea.

BRIAN CLOUGH AT NOTTINGHAM

Manager of Nottingham Forest from 1976 to 1993 winning one League Title, two consecutive European Cups and four League Cups. The City Ground is located right next to the start of the walk at Trent Bridge.

The City Ground, Nottingham

TRENT BRIDGE TO SAWLEY
10.8 miles

Start the walk from Trent Bridge and walk the short distance to the Trent Bridge Inn, go right across two roads and walk down a path to the riverside with Trent Bridge on your right. Now walk away from Trent Bridge, down the riverside with the river on your right. After 500 yards go right over the Suspension Bridge and then left along the embankment with the river on your left.

After ¾ of a mile do not go left over Wilford Toll Bridge but continue straight ahead along Riverside Way. After 400 yards bear left onto Queens Drive and after a further 700 yards go left onto a path waymarked 'Trent Valley Way'. Follow this path under Clifton Bridge and after a further 600 yards join the adjacent road on the right for 100 yards before rejoining the riverside path. Follow this path for 1.5 miles to arrive at Beeston lock.

Victoria Embankment, Nottingham

Cross over to the other side and continue in the same direction. Just past the lock follow the sign to Attenborough. You will now walk next to the river Trent for four and a half miles. Notice the weir to your left then pass in front of the Beeston Marina cafe.

After quarter of a mile pick up the sign 'riverside path to Trent Lock'. In half a mile take the fork left to Trent Lock (you can make a detour if you wish to visit the Attenborough Nature Reserve). After a further half mile take the left path to Trent Lock.

In another half mile you will see the Trent Valley Greenway Loop on your right which is a nice excursion if you have time, otherwise continue towards Trent Lock. After one mile

Beeston Lock

OS © Crown Copyright 2016 GV-215554

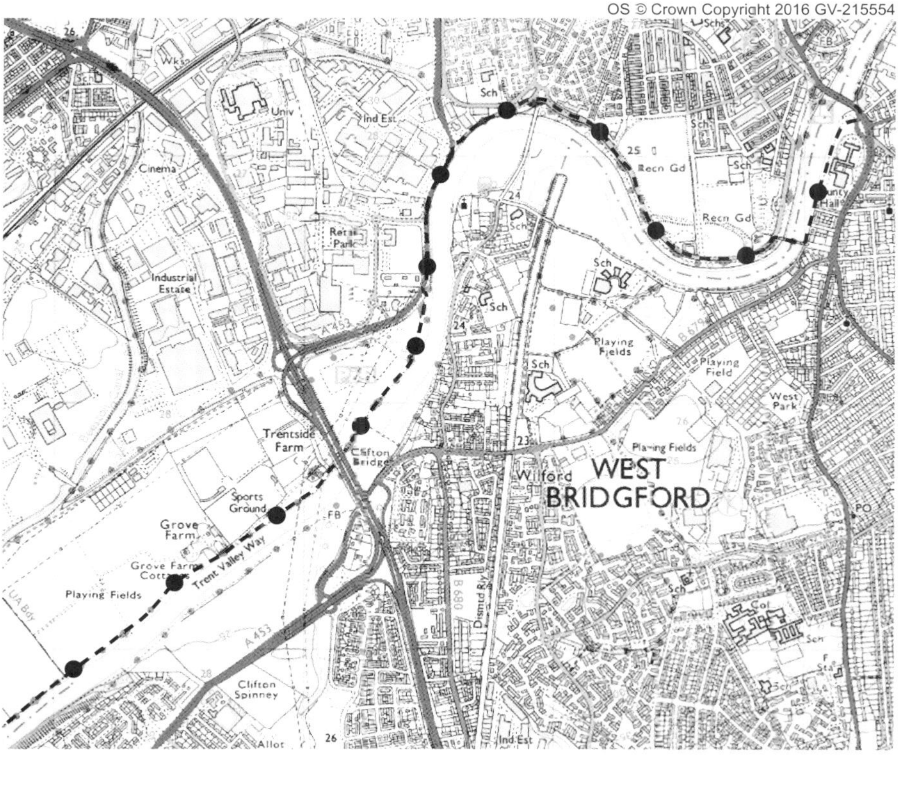

walk past Nottingham Yacht Club and Cranfleet Lock. Walk towards the next lock, under the two railway bridges and up to the lock gates. Rejoin the River Trent with the Trent Valley Sailing Club on the other side of the canal. Continue on the towpath and cross the Erewash Canal via the footbridge. Continue along the path with the river on your left and pass the Navigation Inn on your right.

Proceed for quarter of a mile, pass through a metal gate and after 30 yards turn right down some wooden steps in the side of the flood bank and onto a golf course. Walk across

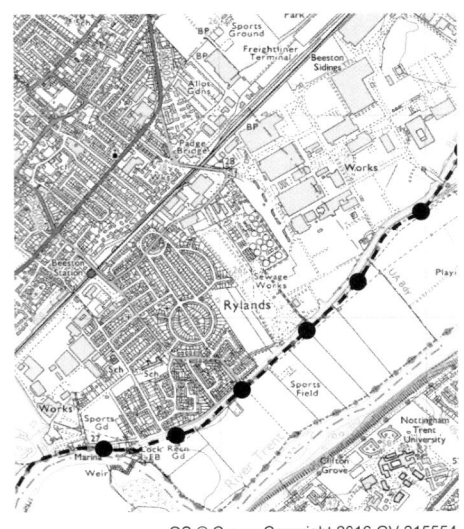

OS © Crown Copyright 2016 GV-215554

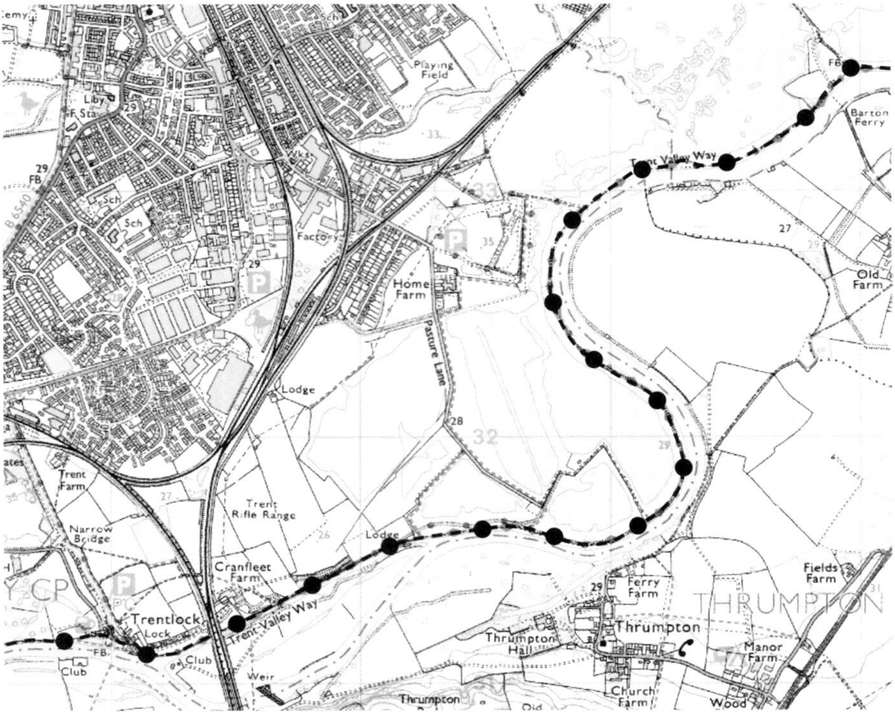

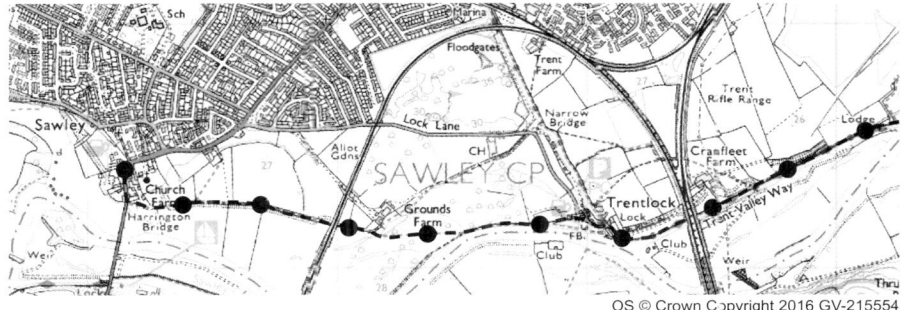

the golf course in the direction of Church Farm on your left. At the other side of the golf course cross a wooden stile and turn left onto the farm track. Pass under a railway bridge and you will see Sawley church on your right and the road bridge on your left. At the bridge come out onto Tamworth road. Cross the road and turn right into Sawley.

SAWLEY TO DERBY
9.6 miles

Just after the White House restaurant turn left into Wilne Avenue, an alleyway between brick walls. After 200 yards come out onto Wilne Road and turn left. Cross over the M1 and after 200 yards turn left into Wilne Lane. After a quarter of a mile go right over a stile signposted 'Midshires Way' (do not take the Bridleway!).

After 500 yards cross a stile in the corner of the field and bear right up onto the floodbank. Keep in the same direction. After a further 400 yards cross two stiles in the same direction (still signposted 'the Midshires Way'). Continue on to meet Wilne Lane again. Cross the lane and go through a metal stile to join a footpath with the River Derwent on your left. The Derwent will now be your companion for the next 55 miles.

After 300 yards Wilne Lane goes to the right but continue on the path between houses and outbuildings to rejoin Wilne Lane on a bend. Walk towards Draycott Village. Turn left into Derwent Street and walk past Draycott

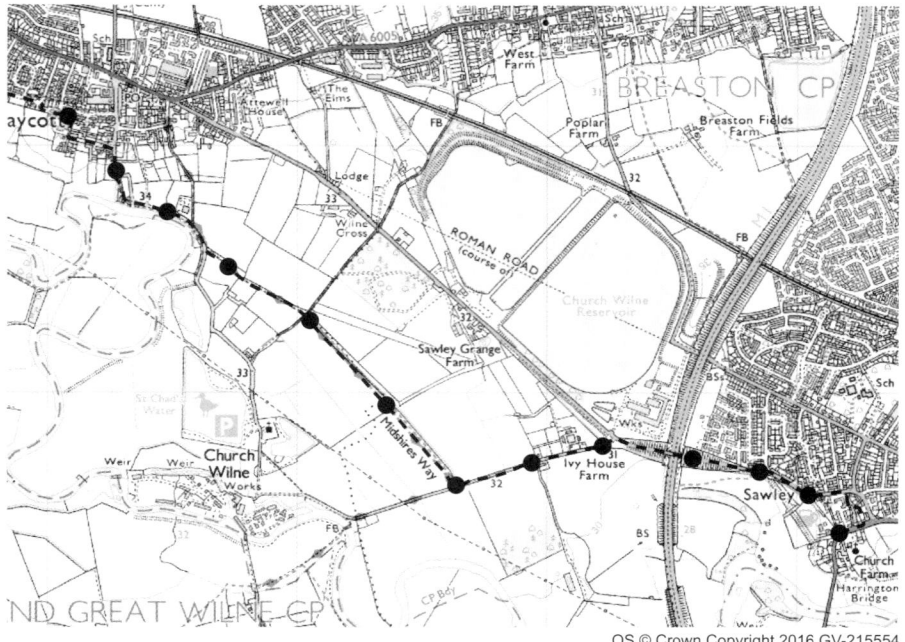

OS © Crown Copyright 2016 GV-215554

Hall. At the end of the street take the footpath on the right then go immediately left and follow the path round the perimeter of a housing estate into a cul-de-sac. Walk from the cul-de-sac round to the left then turn left into Lime Close. After 400 yards, as Lime Close bears right take the path between the houses on the left (this is easily missed).

Cross the stile and go across the middle of a field to woodland opposite. At the end of the woodland cross the bridge and the stile into the next field. Go half right across the field and cross a stile signposted 'circular walk'. Go over another stile and down the edge of a field with the hedge on your left. At the corner go through a squeeze-through stile onto a public bridle way. Turn right and walk 400 yards up the bridleway and over the railway line. At the end of Noonings Lane cross the main road and turn right.

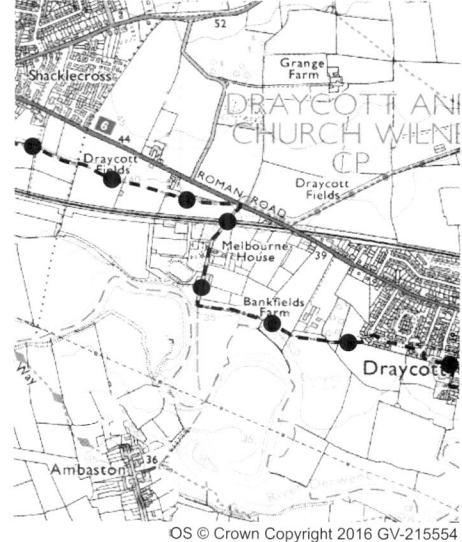

OS © Crown Copyright 2016 GV-215554

Walk along the pavement to a national cycle path sign on the left. Turn left and take the footpath parallel to and back in the same direction you have come from, signed 'Derby six and a quarter miles'. The path passes back under the main road and over a stile. Walk along the righthand side of the field and go over a stile into the next field. Cross a stile and then after 20 yards a stile and a bridge. Walk across the middle of a field and cross a stile

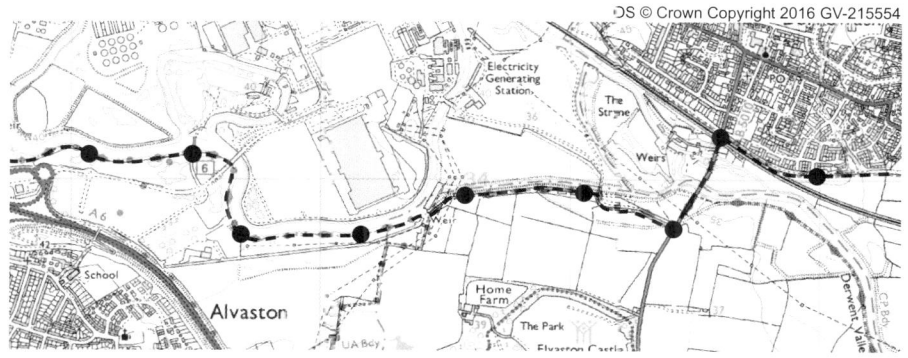

OS © Crown Copyright 2016 GV-215554

25

and a wooden bridge into the next field with a hedge on the left. Pass through two more stiles and a third by a six bar metal gate. Cross onto a track straight ahead. Cross the road to the sub-station, through the gate opposite, and over a delightful wooden bridge.

Go along the cycle path with a housing estate on your right. Walk up onto the road bridge with the Derby Canal path signposted opposite.

Cross the road, do not take the Derby Canal path, turn left and walk down the road over four bridges, the first goes over the railway and the last over the river Derwent. Immediately after the fourth bridge turn right over the stile and follow the path next to the Derwent. You are now following the Derwent Valley Heritage Way and will do so for the next 50 miles to the Ladybower Reservoir.

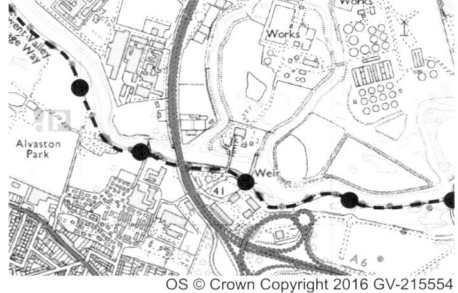

OS © Crown Copyright 2016 GV-215554

The wooden bridge at Borrowash

26

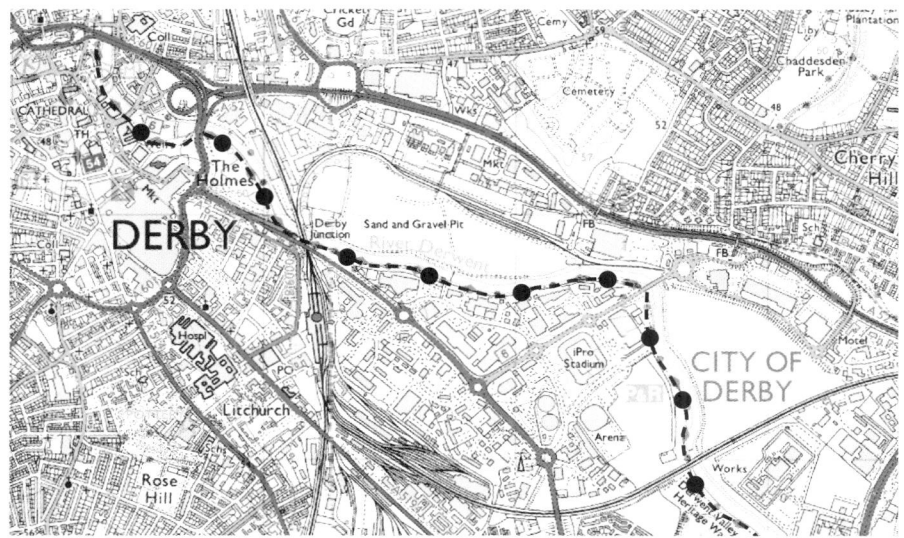

County Hall by the Derwent

Follow the riverside path for 4 miles. This will take you past Pride Park (Derby County F.C.) on the left. Continue towards Derby under the railway beside a road network over a bridge and into a park. When the riverside path is signposted right over the Derwent, ignore this and go straight ahead on the left of the river signposted 'City centre and Riverside Park'. Walk along the left bank of the river, under the road, past the weir and council offices and climb the steps up to the bridge.

BRIAN CLOUGH AT DERBY

Brian was Manager of Derby County from 1967 to 1973, winning one Second Division Title, one League Title and reaching the semi-finals of the European Cup.

Derby County moved from the Baseball Ground to Pride Park in 1997. The walk passes Pride Park.

Statue at the site of the Baseball Ground

A short detour to the other side of the stadium will take you to the Brian Clough and Peter Taylor statue.

For those who wish to visit the original site of the Baseball Ground
¾ of a mile after passing Pride Park, and just before the path and the river go underneath the railway line, bear left away from the river. Pass under a low bridge and climb steps to emerge onto Railway Terrace, opposite the Alexandra Hotel. Turn left and walk along Railway Terrace towards the railway station. On arriving at the station follow the road round to the right which then becomes Midland Road. Walk up to the T-junction at London Road, the A5194, and turn left. Just before the railway bridge bear right into Bateman Street. Follow this up to the T-junction at Osmaston Road, the A514, and turn left. Take the third road on the right which is Shaftesbury Road. Walk up the road and when it turns left go right into Colombo Street. At the end of Colombo Street walk into Baseball Drive. This is the site of the Baseball Ground and to your right you will see the commemorative statue. (Distance 1.2 miles)

DERBY TO BELPER
8.5 miles

Cross the road and continue on the riverside path past the Derby Silk Mill and under Handyside Bridge. At this point do not turn back up onto the bridge but continue past Derby Boat Club through Darley Park and past the wildlife area. At the cricket pitch leave the river briefly and bear left to Darley Abbey Village.

Turn right through the village past the Abbey but when you reach 'Square' on your left turn right and rejoin the riverside path in a park area. At the end of Old Lane cross the old toll bridge and into the mill car park. Walk out of Darley Mill and into Haslams Lane.

On reaching Derby Rugby Club turn left between two rugby pitches signed 'Heritage Way'. As the track turns right into a car park carry straight on over the stile into fields with the river on your left. After 200 yards bear right across the field to rejoin the river on a bend. After a further 100 yards the river leaves you to the left so proceed straight on over a stile and into fields of lawn turf.

Follow the Heritage waymarkers across the fields to a bridge under the A38. Walk under the bridge and then take the steps on your right back up to the A38.

At the top of the steps turn left, walk over the railway and take the

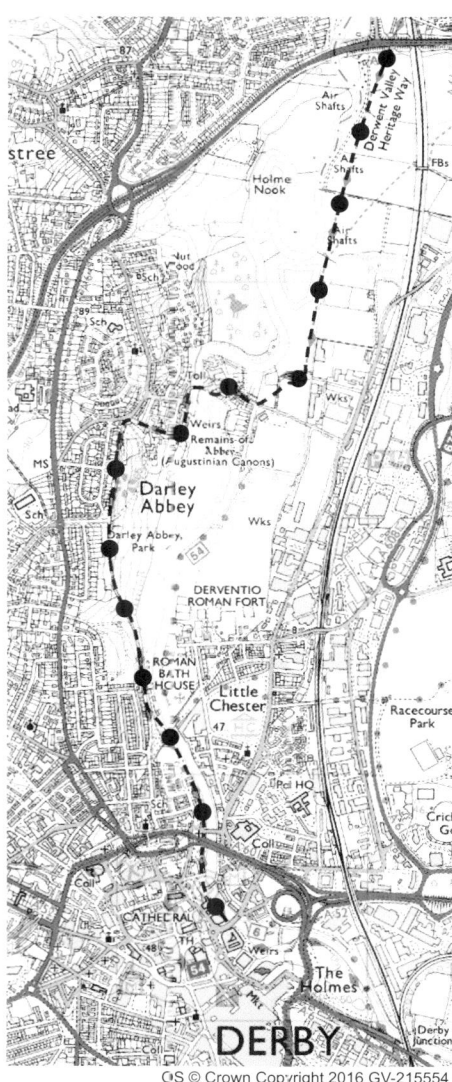

OS © Crown Copyright 2016 GV-215554

31

steps down on your left signposted 'Ford Lane'. On meeting Ford Lane turn right and walk up to the roundabout. At the roundabout take the cycle path left to Little Eaton.

On entering Little Eaton take the road bearing left to Duffield. After quarter of a mile turn right up Church Lane and at the top turn left into Vicarage Lane. At Greenbank House go left over the stile in the stone wall. Continue to follow the Heritage Way signs through a wood, over a stone walled bridge and down a slope to the right. At the bottom make an oblique turn left down to the Duffield road.

Turn right up the road and walk along to Derwent House on your left. Turn left down the track next to the gated road and follow the walled path into the field and onto Duffield Bridge.

Leave the Heritage Way at this point by going left over the river and railway line before turning immediately right down steps to a field. Cross diagonally left across this field to the far left corner and emerge onto the A6. Turn right and walk through Duffield for ¾ of a mile passing the Kings Arms and Railway Station on your right.

On reaching Avenue Road on your left leave the A6 by bearing left down a footpath waymarked 'Public footpath to Chevin' that almost immediately brings you to Chevin Golf Club on your right. Walk up the road and then go right, round the back of the clubhouse, and follow the track ahead with the golf course still on your right. After 400 yards the track goes through the middle of the golf course. Do not take this but go left over a stile and then over a second stile. The path then bears right with the golf course on both sides and then climbs a hill.

Three quarters of the way up the hillside the path bears left behind a golf tee and continues up the hill. Don't forget to look at the retrospective views

32

The path through Chevin Golf Course

across the valley. Go through a wall and then the path bears right and then immediately left to continue climbing the hillside with a wall on your left. After a steep climb come to a four-way junction. Go straight ahead up the hill crossing another path on the way to the top. Go through a stone squeeze-through stile onto a wider track and turn left. Follow this wide track between walls for one mile with lovely views on your right across the Derwent Valley. After one mile go right down the left hand side of a field downhill towards Belper. Halfway down go over a wooden stile and eventually emerge onto Chevin Road. Turn left and walk along the road for 150 yards before taking a well established path on the right in front of houses. At the end of the houses go over the wooden stile and turn left down the hill. At the bottom of the hill go through a stone squeeze stile in a hedge and come out onto a path next to the river. Turn left and follow the path for ½ a mile with

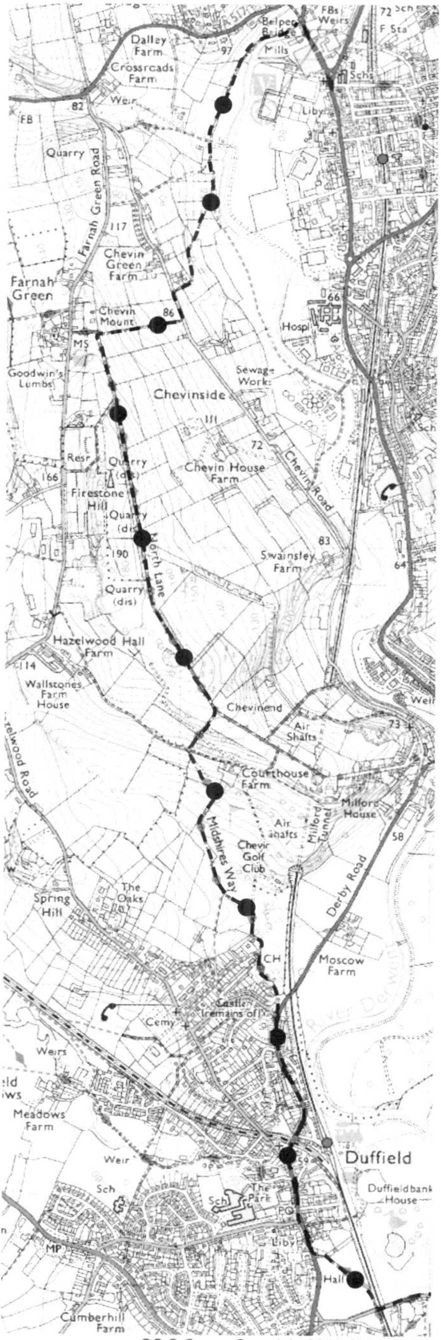

CS © Crown Copyright 2016 GV-215554

the river on your right. Arrive at Belper Bridge. Start your next day by following the instructions from Belper after you have crossed the Derwent with the weir on you right.

The River Derwent at Belper

BELPER TO MATLOCK
10.5 miles

From Belper Bridge leave the A517 and turn right into Bridgefoot. After 30 yards bear right into Wyver Lane. Pass Wyver Lane Pool on your right, a nature reserve. Do not take the bridleway left but continue along the lane. At a metal farm gate bear left for 30 yards to a squeeze-through stile next to a metal gate indicating 'Lawn Cottage'.

Walk 200 yards across the field to come to a waymarker signposted 'Whitewells Road'. Bear left for 20 yards and cross a stone stile to the left of a wooden gate. Continue up the field skirting the wood on your left. Do not be drawn towards the farm on the right but continue up the field to the top. Go over a stone stile between a wooden fence and walk up the next field with a wood on your right. Cross the high stone stile in the right hand corner onto Whitewells Road.

The weir at Belper

Turn right and walk along the road for half a mile before turning right down Holly Lane. Walk down the hill, over the Derwent and up to the A6. Turn left and walk along the pavement to the Hurt Arms Hotel in Ambergate. After quarter of a mile turn right into Chase Road. Walk under the railway and climb up to the canal bridge. Take the towpath on the left just before the bridge and stay on this for the next 3 miles.

Half a mile after Whatstandwell walk through Cromford tunnel. Walk a further half mile, cross the railway line and then cross over to the right of the canal before crossing the aqueduct. At the other side note the Leawood Pump House on your right which has restricted opening times throughout the year. Pass High Peak Junction and stay on the right of the canal.

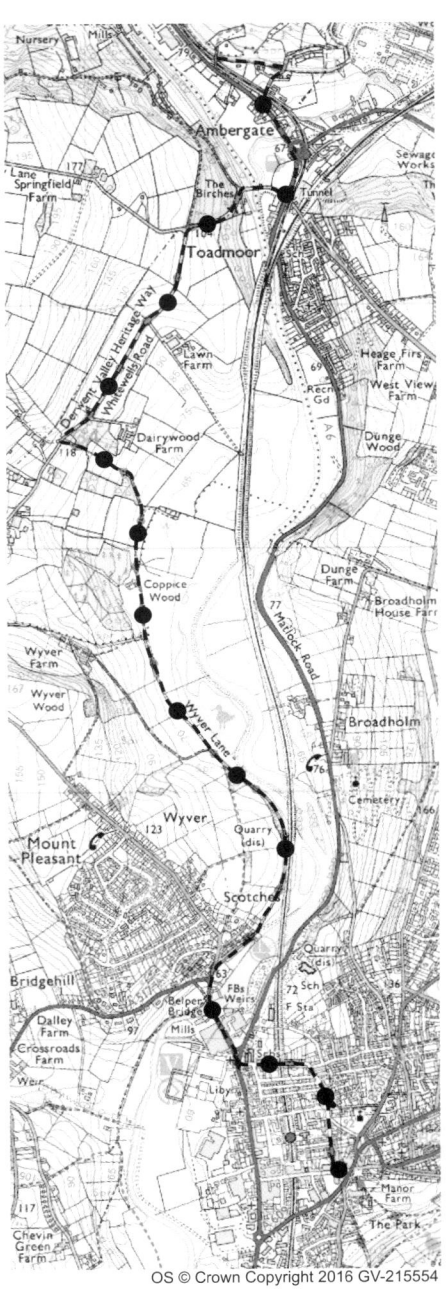

Cromford Canal Aquaduct

OS © Crown Copyright 2016 GV-215554

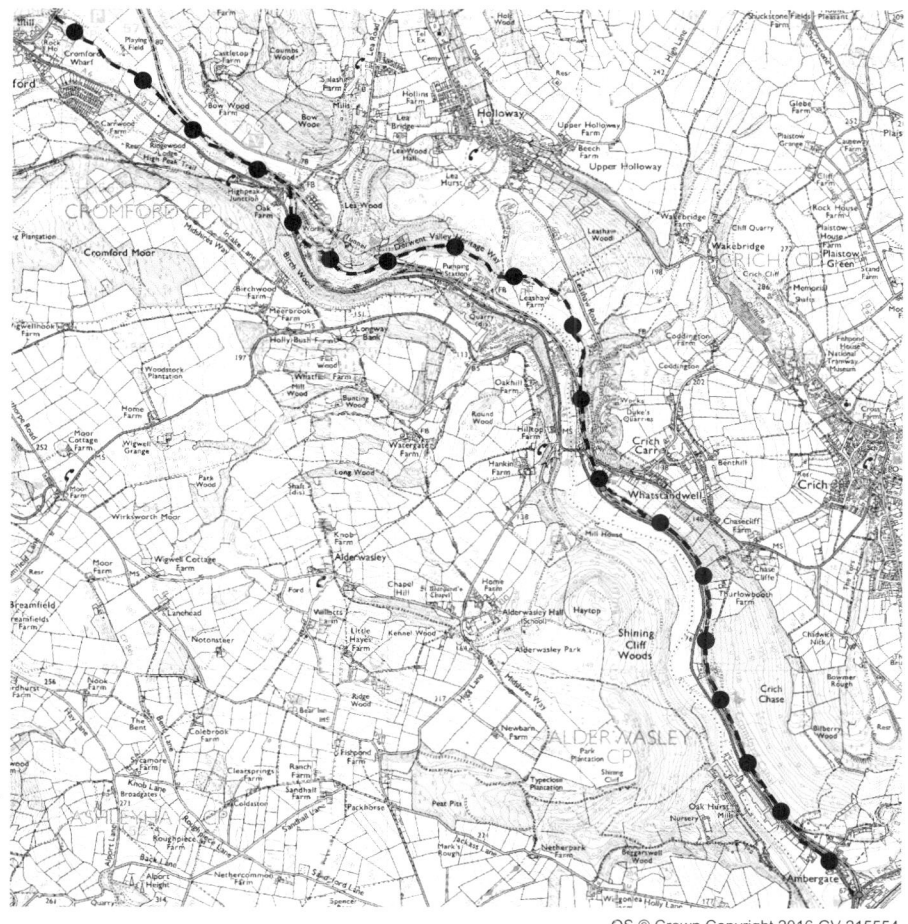

OS © Crown Copyright 2016 GV-215554

Walk past the rugby pitches on the right, go under the canal bridge and walk on to the end of the canal. Cross the road and enter the car park for Sir Richard Arkwright's Cromford Mills. Leave by the path in the bottom left hand corner. With the river on your right walk up to the A6.

Turn right and walk past Masson Mills to Matlock Bath. Walk on the A6 through Matlock Bath and at the end of the shops go right across the road bridge to the station. Follow the signs to High Tor over the railway line and up past the cable car station. High Tor offers magnificent views over Matlock Bath Gorge. Descend from High Tor and at the exit gates to High Tor Park

37

turn left downhill and go under a railway bridge. Turn right (do not cross the river) and after 400 yards cross Bentley Brook on your left. Turn left and walk on the right of the Derwent to the end of Hall Leys Park. Cross left over the road bridge to the traffic lights.

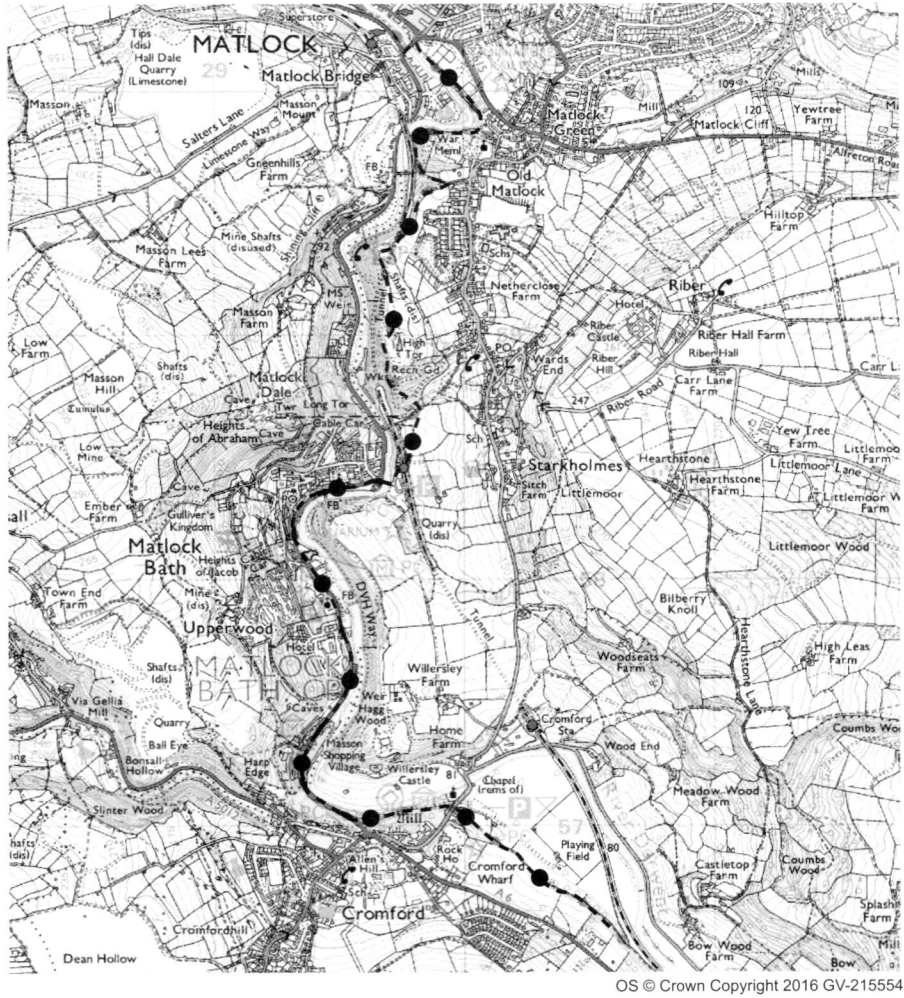

MATLOCK TO BASLOW
9.2 miles

Turn right at the traffic lights and follow the pedestrian path next to the river. Now enjoy a delightful walk on the left hand side of the river. Ascend from the river and pass a stoneworks on your left. A quarter of a mile further on cross a stile next to the river waymarked 'Heritage Way'. Skirt the right edge of a field with the river on your right and pass through a squeeze-through stile.

Walk through the middle of a field, through an open gate, and along the right edge of the next field with the village of Oker on the hillside to your left. Walk up a path with a hedge on either side. Come out onto Aston Lane and turn right. After 400 yards come to a metal gate and pass through the stile next to it. Follow this gated road across a field, throught another gate, between houses, past allotments, and up to Darley Bridge. Turn right and

Matlock

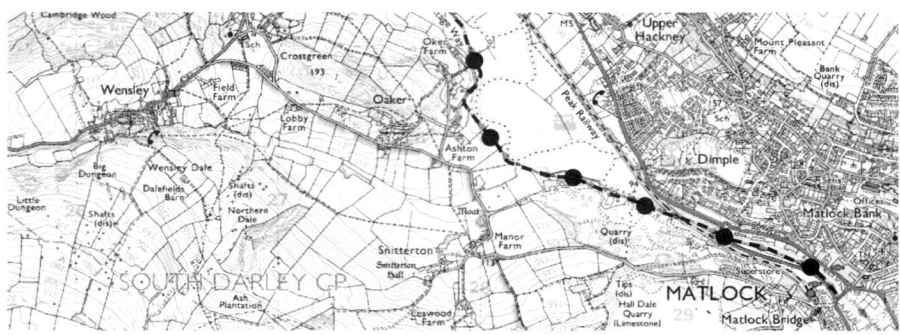

OS © Crown Copyright 2016 GV-215554

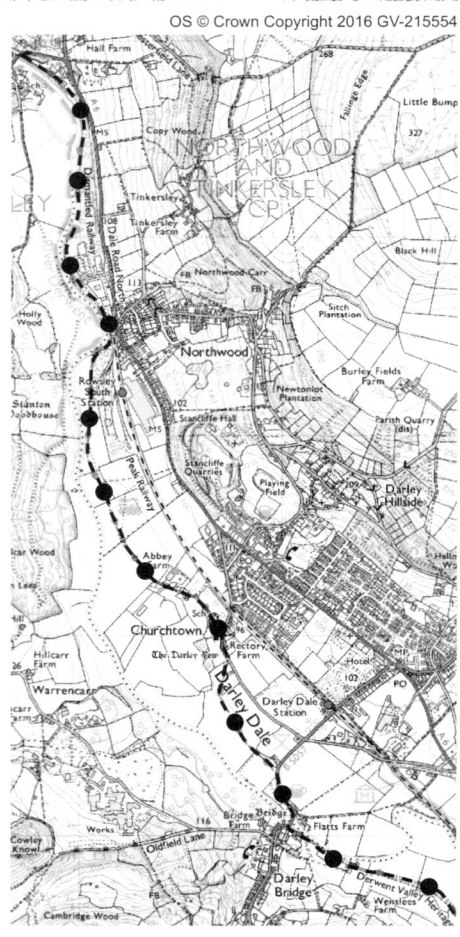

cross the bridge following the pavement round to the cricket ground on your left. Take the path on the left passing alongside the cricket ground. Follow the path on the right of a field with a stream on your right. At the end of the field turn right over a bridge crossing the stream and through a metal gate. Go across the middle of the field ahead. On reaching the road turn left and walk past the church. Follow the next road on the left past the Darley Churchtown C of E Primary School and walk through the gates labelled Abbey House and Abbey Farm. Pass between a group of houses and towards the open fields. Do not turn right towards the stables but continue through the squeeze-through stile next to the gate and go straight on. Go over the stone step stile next to another metal gate and into the field.

You now follow a series of stiles and fields until you come to a path on the right of the river. On arriving at the end of the railway line do not cross towards the A6 but proceed to

Chatsworth House

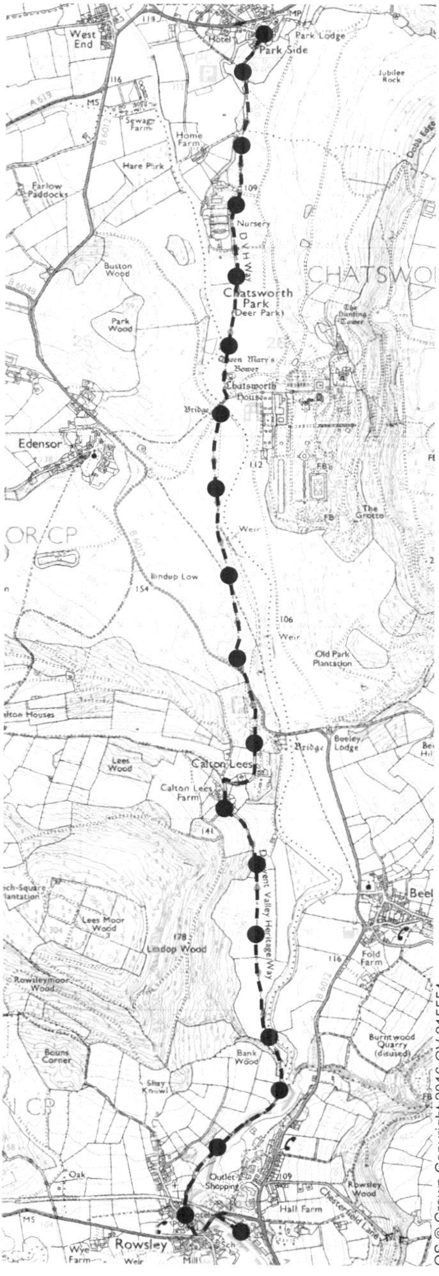

your left. Walk into a turning area with a signpost on the left to Peak Rail. Walk straight across, and bear right between stone posts onto a path through the woods. After half a mile come out onto a road next to a factory complex. Turn left and follow the road round to the A6. On emerging from Old Station Close cross the A6 carefully and go left over the river and past the Grouse and Claret.

Just past The Peacock turn right into Church Lane. After 200 yards turn right onto a dirt track and under a bridge. This eventually emerges into fields and woodland . Follow this path with the river on your right. After about a mile you will walk across the middle of two wide fields. At a third field follow the path up to your left with woodland on your left. At the top of the hill cross over the wall on the left via the ladder stile and turn right.

Make your way down to the beautiful village of Carlton Lees. Enter the village via the stile on your right and walk down to the triangular grass island. Take the road on the right and walk past the back of the garden centre and over the road by a white fenced cattle grid. You are now walking towards Chatsworth House with the river on your right.

At Chatsworth House cross the ornate road bridge and then turn immediately left.

After 20 yards go through a wooden gate and follow the path past the right hand side of the cricket pitch. Note the thatched roof on the pavilion. On the approach to Baslow go through a very distinctive kissing gate. At Plantation Cottage do not go left across the field but continue on the path. Come to a blue gate with a squeeze-through stile to the right of it onto the road. At the end of the road turn left over the bridge into Baslow.

BASLOW TO HEATHERDENE
11 miles

Walk past the toilets of the left and then cross the main road coming from your right and enter Eaton Road. At the top of Eaton Road bear left into School Lane and walk back down to the main A623 at the mini roundabout. Turn right and then left at the Rutland Arms to Bubnell.

Cross the bridge and then turn right with the river now on your right. Pass Bubnell Grange on your left. Do not turn left but continue on the road in the same direction. At the bottom of the hill follow the Heritage Way sign diagonally across a field to your right. Pass through a gate and follow the path with a wall on your right hand side. The path eventually enters woodland and rejoins the river on your right. Continue next to the river to Calver and walk under the underpass to the other side.

Church at Bubnell

At the road next to the old bridge turn left and then immediate right to Newbridge and Froggat. Do not turn right into Calver Mill but carry on to Stocking Farm. Pass to the right of the farm through a gate and diagonally across a field towards the river. Follow the farm track into the trees. Go through a six bar metal gate and continue into the woods. Eventually walk out of the trees, pass two bungalows on your left and up to the road. Cross the road and through the gate opposite way-marked Heritage Way.

After 200 yards cross the bridge over the stream and continue on the path round to the right. At the next bridge over the river pass through the gate onto the road and turn right to cross the bridge into Froggatt.

At the other side turn left into Hollowgate. At Rose Cottage continue straight on up Spooner Lane which eventually becomes a path between walls. 30 yards past a metal gate, where the wall ends on the right, cross diagonally right and then bear left through an opening into a field. Eventually cross a stone path through the middle of a field to a stile.

You now enter Froggat Wood. Walk through the wood and at the other side walk down a hill with a wall on your right to pass through a wooden gate on your right. Bear right across a field to the far corner by the bridge in Grindleford.

Turn Right and after 100 yards, just before Riverbank House, go

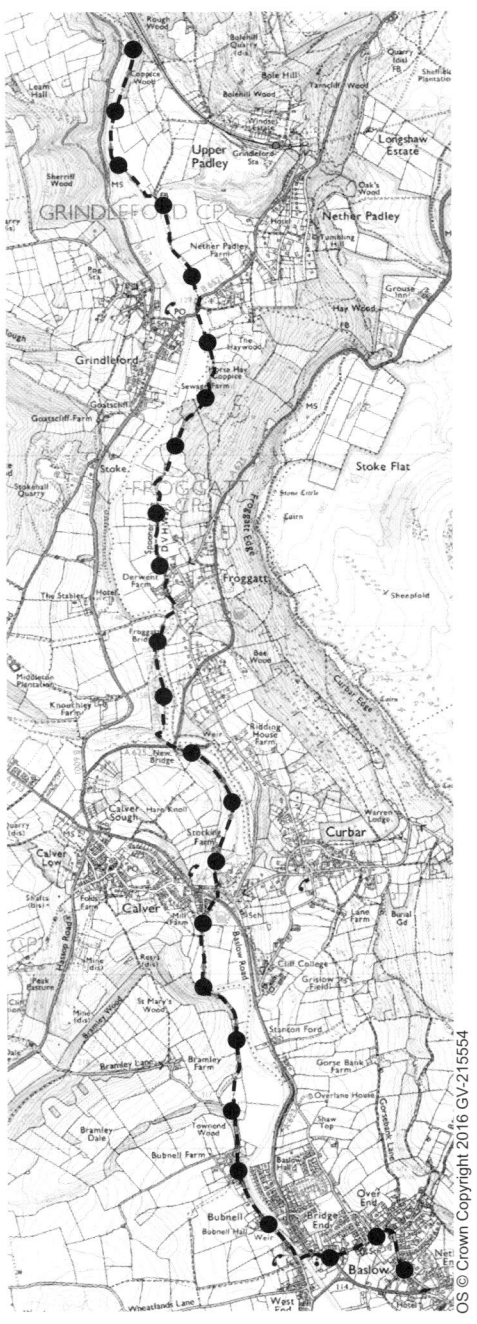

The bridge at Froggatt

through a gate on your left into a field next to the river. After quarter of a mile negotiate a creek by leaving the river, crossing a bridge, and then returning to the riverside. After a couple of miles come out onto a lane and turn left still with the river on your left hand side. At the end of the lane, where it meets the main road to Hathersage, turn left and cross Leadmill Bridge.

Leadmill Bridge

At the other side of the bridge cross the road and pass through the squeeze-through stile waymarked 'Heritage Way' and signposted to Shatton. After a short distance walk through a wood next to the river and cross a wooden bridge. After a mile come to some stepping stones signposted to

Castleton Road. Do not cross them but continue on the left bank of the river signposted to Shatton.

Pass down into a wooded area and over a wooden bridge. Go out of the wooded area into a wide field. Walk on the right of the field next to the river. Pass through woodland with a steep drop to the river on your right. Eventually come out onto a road. Turn right and walk round to the main road. Cross over and go through the gate signposted to Thornhill and Yorkshire Bridge. Walk down the left hand side of the garden centre car park and under the railway bridge in the corner. Immediately turn left through a small gate into a field. Follow the left hand edge of the field round to a large house called 'Derwent Valley Water Board'.

Climb over the stile into the lane and turn left to Yorkshire Bridge and

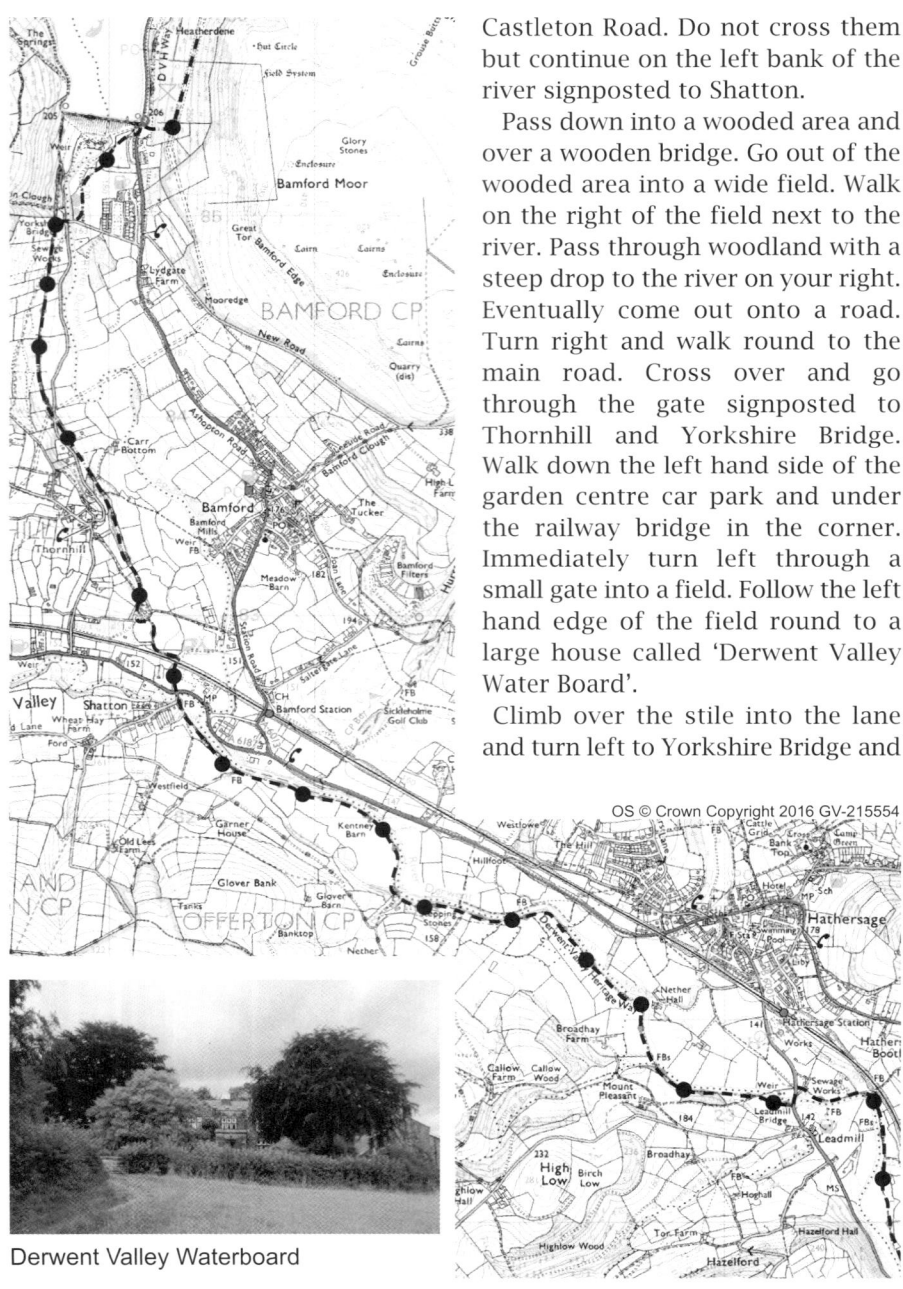

OS © Crown Copyright 2016 GV-215554

Derwent Valley Waterboard

Thornhill. Walk a few yards then turn right to access the old railway line. After one mile cross the road to Thornhill and continue on the old railway line. After a further half mile take a right fork down to Yorkshire Bridge.

Cross the bridge and then take the path left to Heatherdene.

On reaching the Ladybower Dam cross the road to a 'Derwent Valley Waterboard' monument. Ascend the steps and walk through the picnic area to the Heatherdene car park. At the end of the path go through a gate with the toilets on your right.

Lady Bower Dam from Heatherdene

HEATHERDENE TO LANGSETT
12.5 miles

Continue to walk north through the car park and then left down to the main road. Turn right and walk over the bridge to the traffic lights.

Turn left on the A57 and walk up to where the road crosses the reservoir. Just before the reservoir go through a gate on the right. You will now walk 6 miles down the east side of the Ladybower, Derwent and Howden reservoirs passing the impressive Derwent and Howden dams.

Towards the end of your 6 miles Howden reservoir becomes a river. Continue on the path to the right of the river. At Derwent Bridge do not cross the river but continue to bear right past the signpost to Langsett. Do not take the oblique cycle path right but continue on to the wooden footbridge. Cross the footbridge and turn right.

At the sign that indicates 'Walkers Only' to the left take the bridleway right. This split occurs at the Howden Moor sign. Follow the bridleway as it meanders its way up the hillside. The path eventually is less stony and

Howden Dam

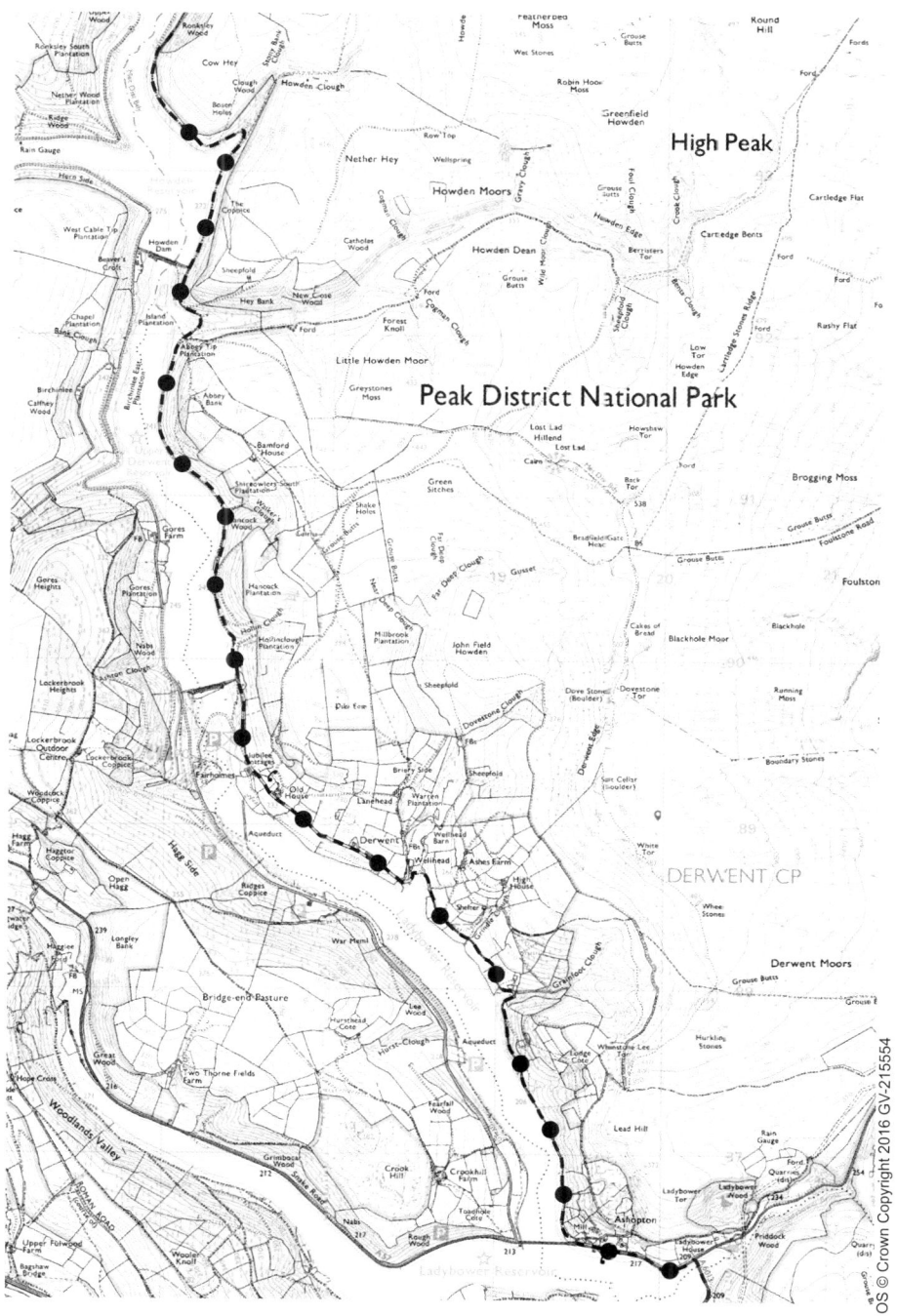

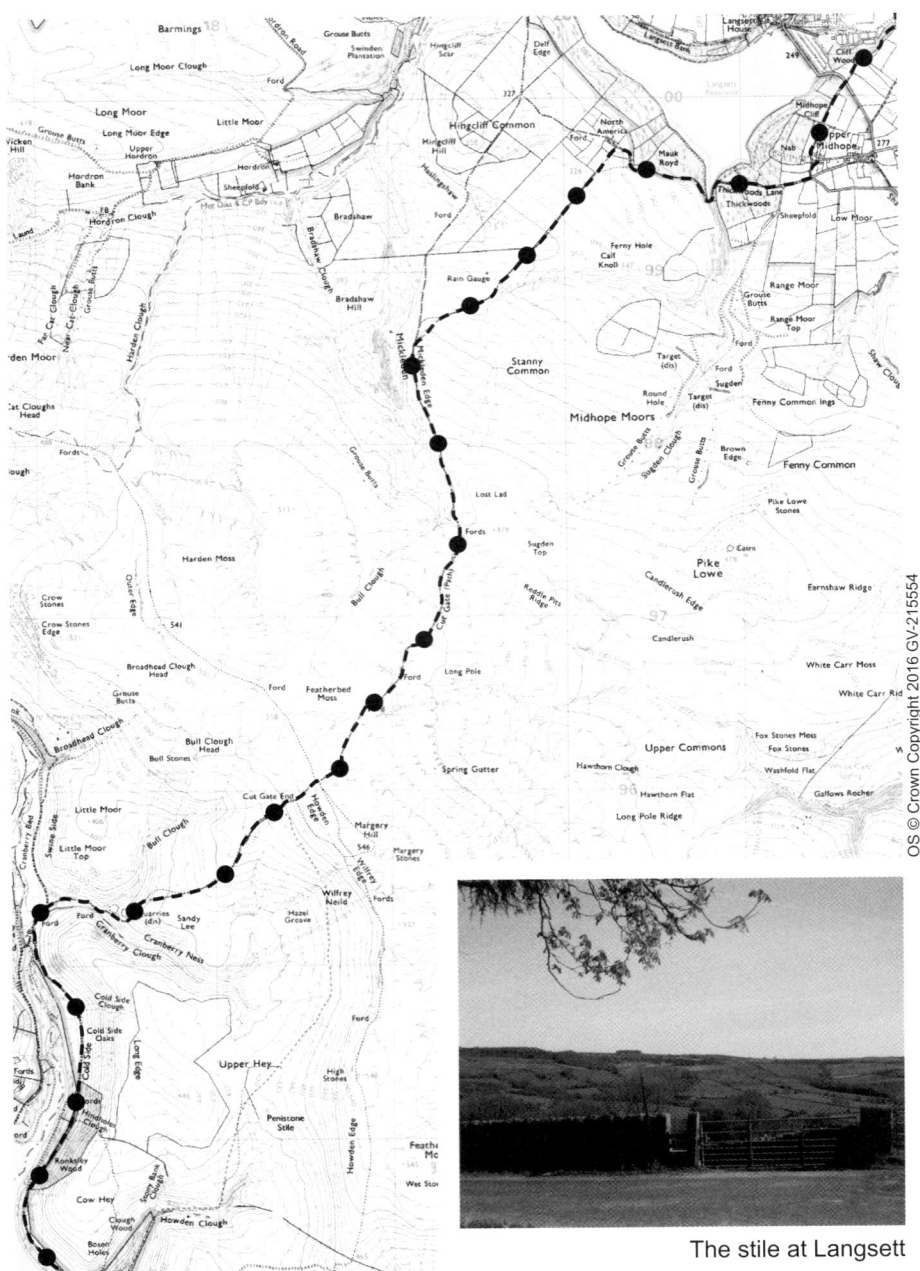

The stile at Langsett

50

becomes a soil vehicle track rising in a north easterly direction towards Howden Edge. Proceed across the moors at the top and down the gradual slope on the other side with the A628 on the horizon in the distance. Eventually bear right at a sign to Langsett and Peniston.

After walking a further half mile the Langsett Reservoir can be seen directly in front of you. The path now follows a dry stone wall on your left. When the wall reaches a five-bar gate do not pass through the gate but follow the track down to the right. This descends gradually with a fence on your left which borders a coniferous wood. At the bottom of the hill you encounter the reservoir. Just cross the bridge and follow the path round to the left. Pass through a six-bar metal gate. Leave the reservoir and take the path curving round to the right. At the top of the hill go through a metal gate and continue straight on the concrete road. After 300 yards do not take the road to the right to 'Derwent Valley' but take the path to the left between two stone walls. On reaching a road turn right for 30 yards then follow the public footpath to the right to where it meets a gravel road. Continue on this gravel road. When the forest on your left ends you will meet a road.

Cross this road and go over the stile opposite. Proceed down through the field, through another gate and after 50 yards go over a stone stile on your left to join a public footpath down through the wood. This gives way to a beautiful wooded walk with a stream down to your left hand side. Eventually emerge from the wood by crossing a broken stone stile. Turn immediately left, cross the bridge and walk up to the A616.

LANGSETT TO CLAYTON WEST
8.5 miles

Turn right and walk along the A616 for 200 yards. Just before Porters Brook Lodge, Greenfield Cottage and Springfield cross the stile on the left and cut diagonally back across a field towards a disused railway line. Do not take the public bridleway.

Cross the railway line and climb through four fields to Nether House. Cross the drive and go through a gate into a field. Cross the middle of the field and climb over the wall onto a farm track. Take this opportunity to look back over Langsett reservoir and Howden Moor.

Turn right through a farmyard with dwellings on the left. Continue on the farm track heading north. At the next farm gate turn left and walk down to the road. Turn right and walk up the road for 200 yards. Take the public bridleway on the left and enjoy a balcony walk around Hartcliffe Hill. This eventually emerges into a field and then becomes a walled downhill path. On reaching a road turn right between houses and walk up the road for 400 yards.

The path down to Thurlston

Take a public footpath left between three metal posts and down steps. Pass through two more sets of metal posts and emerge onto a farm track leading right down to the Trans Pennine Way. Turn right onto the Trans Pennine Way and after 100 yards go left down steps and over a bridge into a yard. Turn right and after 50 yards take the public footpath to the left, between stone walls, eventually leading to the A628 in the middle of Thurlston.

Cross the A628 and walk up to the right past Hollybank Cottage and

Scout Dyke Reservoir

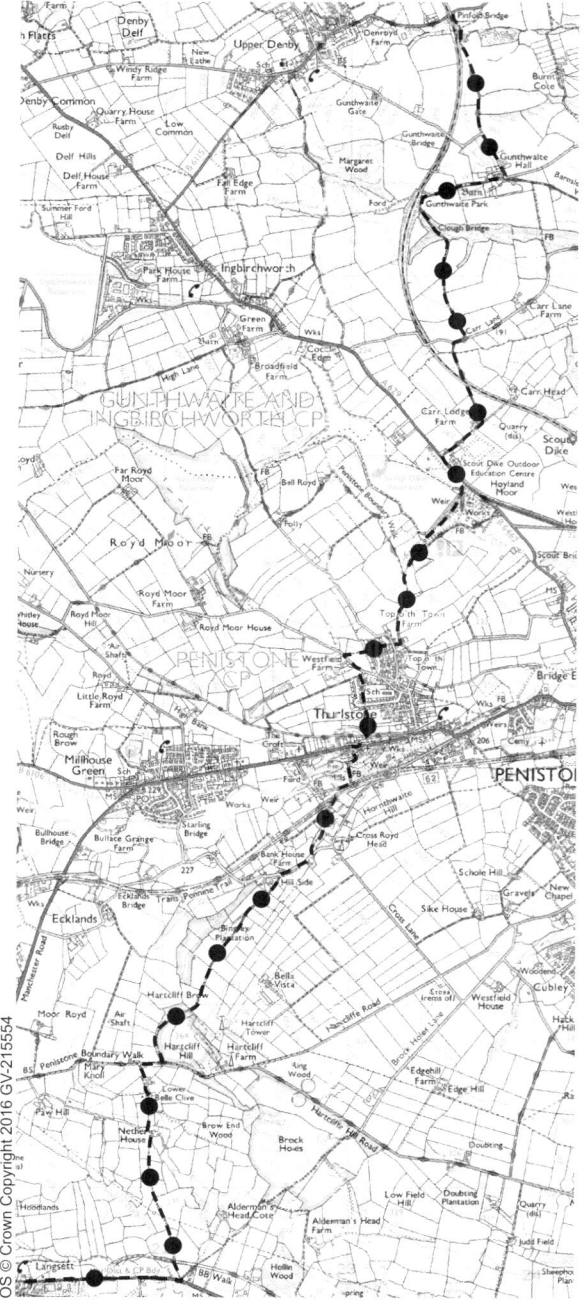

Edgehill House. At the top of the lane turn right and then immediately left up stone steps to follow the public footpath. Go through a turnstile and past a children's playground on your left. Cross a road and pass a school playing field on your right. On reaching Westfield Lane turn right and then immediately left past Westfield Loft. Just past Westfield Farm take a public footpath at right angles to the right across a field to a bungalow. Go over the wall, through the garden of the bungalow and walk down Kensington Avenue.

At the bottom turn right down a dirt track and then right again in front of a bungalow named Stonehaven.

After 200 yards bear left into a field then right along the edge of the field. At the corner of the field turn left up the field with a stone wall on your right. At the top of the hill go over the wall on your right and walk down towards the Scout Dyke.

Go over a metal stile on the right and then immediately left through the wood a short distance to the reservoir. Turn right and walk along the grassy path on top of the dam. At the end of the dam climb left up the steps to the car park. Walk through the car park and emerge onto the A629 opposite the Peak Activities Centre.

Cross the A629 Halifax Road and walk left a short distance before turning right down a public bridleway. You are now on the Peniston Boundary Walk. Continue down hill past the entrance to the activities centre and just past a farm turn left down a path to a railway line. Cross the railway line with care and then after a short distance emerge onto a lane. Turn right and after 100 yards go left down a public footpath. Walk down the right hand side of several fields and eventually bear left through a gate into a wood. Follow the track through the wood and in doing so cross the dilapidated but aptly named Clough Bridge.

Emerge from the wood and follow the track round to the right to Gunthwaite Farm. Walk through the farm buildings (which includes Gunthwaite Hall) and turn left onto Gunthwaite Lane. At the next bend do not follow the lane round to the left but continue straight on into the field. Hugging the right hand side, pass through a gate and after 100 yards leave the edge of the field and go straight across heading for the Holmefirth Beacon on the horizon. Half way across the field pass a tree with a waymarker and proceed to the bottom left hand corner by the railway embankment.

Go down into a wooded area and out of the other side via wooden steps. Descend some stone steps to a road and turning right walk the short distance into Lower Denby.

Follow the road round to the left past The Old School House and up to the junction at the A635. Cross the A635 and walk up the road on the right of the Dunkirk Inn. There is a telephone box opposite the Dunkirk Inn where you could ring for a taxi for accommodation. Walk up the road past Tinter House Farm on your left. After ½ a mile at Exley Gate turn left with the Holmefirth Mast now at 11 o'clock. After 200 yards go straight on down Clough House Lane. Follow this past Clough House Lodge but after a further ¼ of a mile, when the track turns right at Clough House, go straight on through the kissing gate and onto Bagden Park Golf Course. Walk to the right of the 18th Tee and walk down the line of trees to the bottom of the golf course. (The trees are marked with faint white circles to indicate the right of way.)

Emerge from the golf course onto a track and take the public footpath opposite. You are now on the Kirklees Way. This will be your companion for 15 miles and is often waymarked by a Blue 'K' under a Yellow arrow which appears on lamp posts and walls. Go down past the muddy pond on your

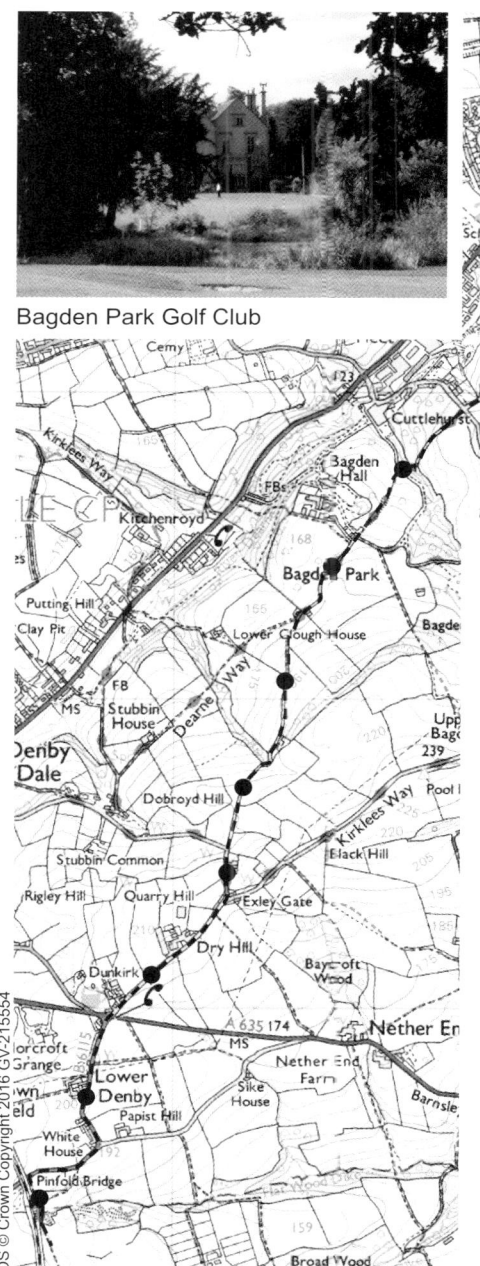

Bagden Park Golf Club

right, up to the stone wall and turn left to walk up through a wood and along a track. Cross a road into Lower Common Lane. After ¼ of a mile come to houses and bungalows on your left. 200 yards before the T-junction turn right up a very narrow path between a stone wall and a fence.

At the end of the path go over a stone wall into a field. Walk up the left side of the field to a wooden stile by a broken metal gate. Cross the stile and walk down the left hand side of the next field. Where the edge of the field meets a wood go over the stile, do not take the path left into a field but go right, down the steps and into the wood. Cross the clapper bridge at the bottom of the wood and walk up the steep slope on the left of the next field. At the top left hand corner

55

step over a very low stone stile, do not take the steps to the right but carry on straight ahead through the wood. Eventually come out into a small car park with the bowling club on your right. Exit at the top right corner of the car park down a path with a stone wall on the left and a metal fence on your right. Bear left by some garages onto Homefield Close and continue straight ahead for 300 yards into Clayton West.

Clayton West

CLAYTON WEST TO BATLEY
14.5 miles

Turn right into Church lane and walk to the bottom to the T-junction. Cross the road and turn right to walk up the road. Between the bus stop and the village stores turn left down a narrow alleyway between the store wall and a brick wall.

Pass through a metal kissing gate and cross the middle of a field to a stile. Go over this stile and cross a second field to a stile. Go over this stile and bear right with hedge on your right. Cross a wooden bridge and a stile and walk up another field.

At the top right hand corner cross a stile and bear right across a small field. Cross a stile and continue up the middle of the next field. You can see a church in the trees on Hoyland Bank to your right. Go over the stile in the top left hand corner and walk along the left edge of the next field. Cross a stile onto the corner of a road. Walk left down the road into the valley towards the A636 with the sewage farm on your left hand side. At the bottom of the hill cross the River Dearne via the stone bridge.

Cross the A636, go through the metal gate and walk up the track to the left of a field. In the top left hand corner go over a stile next to a gate. Three quarters of the way up the next field, do not carry straight on towards White Cross Farm but leave the main track and go over a stile on the right. Now pass over a series of stiles and fields to reach Woodhouse Farm at the top of the hill. Proceed to

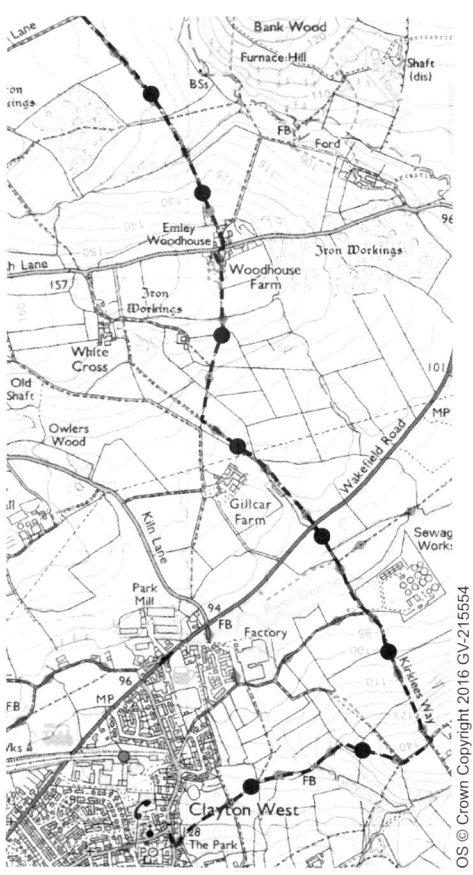

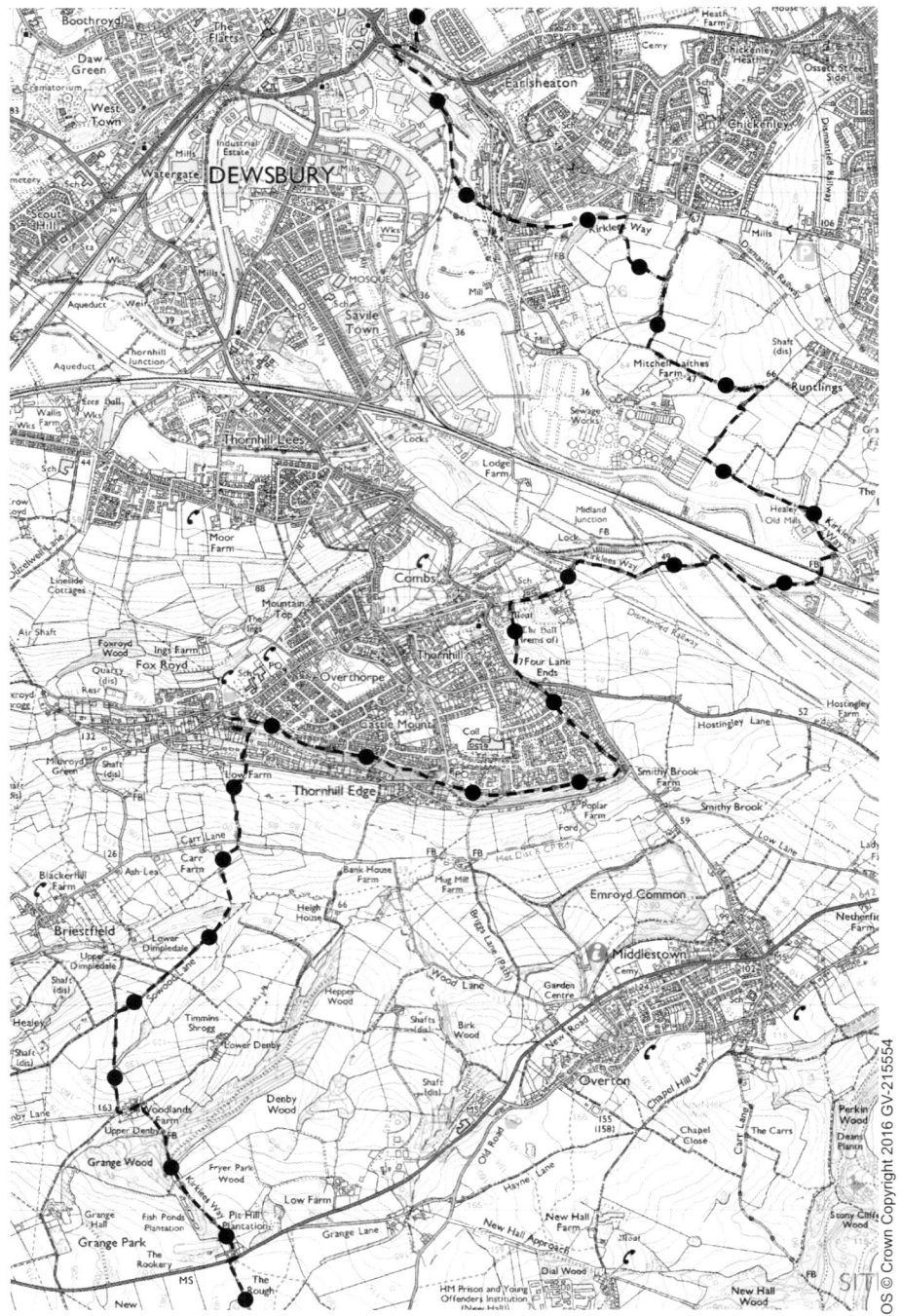

the left of the barn and go over a stile into an area of caravans. Turn right into the farm yard and walk round to the left to Ash Lane. Cross the lane and walk into the drive of Emley Woodhouse Cottage. Do not turn right into the cottage but proceed straight ahead onto a path between nettles and brambles.

Go down a hill into a field and walk round its left edge. At the bottom left corner go through the hedge (easy to miss!) and descend to Little Dike. Walk up the right hand side of the next field. Go over the stile at the top right corner and walk up the next field with a wooden posted fence on your right and then a hedge. Cross a stile and walk up the right hand side of the next field. Go over the next stile and walk diagonally across Leisure Lane to cross another stile. Again walk down the right hand side of the next field.

The Holmefirth Beacon is now very close to you on your left. At the bottom of this field cross over another stile and walk down to Clough Dike. Just before the dike go over a stone stile on the right with metal bars across it. Cross the stone clapper bridge over Clough Dike. Walk across the middle of a field bearing slightly to the right towards a marker post in the hedge. Pass through the hedge and turn left. Where the hedge ends turn left and then immediately through a stile on the right. Walk through the middle of the next two fields. Cross a stile onto a concrete road. Do not turn right down the road but walk straight across the middle of the next two fields. Go over a small clapper bridge and a stile. The path now bears right next to trees by Mill Beck.

Eventually go over a stream by a gate at Mill House Farm and walk round to the right on a slabbed path and onto the drive. Walk down the drive and out of the front gate. Turn right and then after the road crosses the beck turn right up a farm track. At the top of the track walk between houses on Elvis Presley Boulevard to emerge onto the A637 at Flockton. Turn left, walk about 300 yards then opposite the Flockton Stores take the public footpath on the right waymarked Kirklees Way. This is a rough path between gardens and a stone wall.

Cross a road and continue between a stone wall and a hedge. At the top emerge from the houses into the right hand side of a field and proceed to a metal gate. Follow a narrow path between a wood and a fence. Go over a stile and walk down the left hand side of a field to the A642. Cross over the A642, turn right, walk 30 yards and then turn left into a driveway with cottages on your left. Go through a gateway in a wall and down to a metal turnstile.

Walk down the left of a small field, over a wooden stile and down the left of the next field on Pithill Plantation. Go over a stile next to a metal gate and walk down to a wood.

Follow the Kirklees waymarkers through the wood, go over a stile and climb the steep grassy bank. Follow the path between a bungalow and a house and emerge onto a lane. Turn left and after 300 yards make an oblique right turn down a steep path to a wooden gate and stile.

Follow this well established path to a 3-way junction. Turn sharp right down what is marked on the map as Sowood Lane and is waymarked Kirklees Way.

Follow this all the way down to it's conclusion at a wooden stile. Go over the stile and down the field to cross the beck at the bottom via a wooden bridge. Having crossed the beck, follow it round to the right into the bottom left corner of a field. Walk up to the top lefthand corner and exit by the path through and round the hedge. Walk a short distance to Carr Lane and cross it. Go down the left side of the field to eventually locate the path between bushes. Follow the path down to Smithy Brook and cross the wooden bridge. Walk up the left side of the field to a lane in front of elevated houses. This is Low Road.

Looking towards Thornhill Edge from Sowood Lane

Thornhill Edge

The next part of the walk really starts at the Flatt Top public house but there are two ways of getting there. The simple way is to turn right up Low Road into Albion Road and the Flatt Top is at the top of the hill on the right hand side.

The more demanding route is well worth the effort and offers some of the finest views on the entire walk. Turn left onto Low Road and then immediately right up an overgrown track between houses. On emerging onto a road walk left for 100 yards and then go right between houses to ascend three flights of steps. (If the track is too overgrown then walk down Low Road to Daleside and walk up Daleside and round to the right to reach the flights of steps.) At the top of the steps turn right and then enjoy a wonderful balcony walk with extensive views over the countryside you have just walked through. After a third of a mile the path arrives at Albion Road opposite the Flatt Top public house.

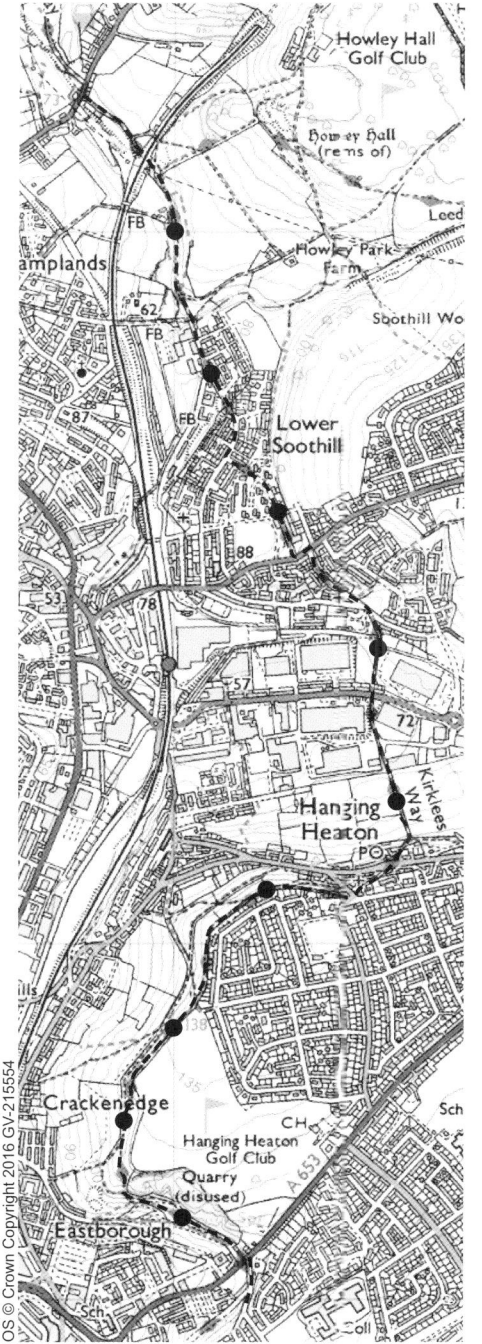

Take the path immediately on the left of the Flatt Top waymarked 'Kirklees Way'. Walk behind houses until the path forks but continue right along Thornhill Edge until it meets a track coming up from the road. Turn left up the track and emerge into Valley Road. Walk to the top of Valley Road and cross the main road to enter a park by a children's play area and toilets. Follow the path to the left through the park and parallel to the main road. On crossing wooden planks with a care home on your left go right and down the park across a grassy area and look for a Kirklees waymarker on a post to your left.

Walk past the post and exit the park via a gap in the wall to arrive on Hall Lane opposite flats. Walk down Hall Lane and through the gates at the bottom.

Pass Thornhill Hall Stables on your right and then go over what looks like a bridge to a T-junction. Turn right and walk down to the Calder and Hebble Navigation Canal. Cross the canal via the Queen Anne Bridge, turn right and walk 500 yards down the towpath. Just before the Lock Keepers Cottage turn left and walk under three railway lines After a short walk across a field cross the beautiful River Calder via a footbridge on your right and come to the entrance of Healey Old Mills on your left.

Walk through the Mills by keeping to the extreme right, next to the wall and within the designated walking area.

61

At the back of the mills exit through a massive green metal kissing gate and walk straight ahead across a field. Enter a second field via a kissing gate to the left of a seven-bar gate and walk straight ahead with a sewage works on your left. On reaching the bottom left hand corner turn right and walk up the left edge of two fields but a third of the way up the second field go through a metal kissing gate on your left.

Bear right for a short distance and then turn left on a narrow path between heather. Walk past a wall on your right and eventually merge onto a wider grassy path. Walk up this track and after 300 yards take the left fork to pass a stone with a Kirklees waymarker. After a short distance take the path on your right on the corner of a copse of trees. At the bottom of the slope after a further 300 yards go left across the middle of a corn field and then follow a narrow track to emerge onto a tarmac cycle track.

Turn left for a third of a mile before walking through a beautifully restored and well lit railway tunnel. At the other side of the tunnel come to a cross roads of paths. Go straight across and the path bears immediately right. Follow this path a short distance to a three-way meeting point with metal artwork and a wooden bench.* Take none of the tarmac tracks but follow a path to the right through a Ridings Wood which emerges into a trailer park. Walk straight across the trailer park, up a short road to arrive at a pelican crossing on the extremely busy Wakefield road.

*At the three way meeting point you may find it more attractive to take the right hand tarmac track into Dewsbury and then walk round to the right to Wakefield Road.

Cross Wakefield Road, turn right and then bear left into Old Bank Road. After 100 yards walk left up Hollinroyd Road and at the top follow a grassy path through to Sugar Lane. Turn left and walk down to the main road. Go over the pelican crossing, turn left and then immediately right down Cualms Wood Road before the Crown Public House. This leads into a beautiful park with a pyramid waymarker. Go right past the pyramid and follow a narrow path through woodland. After about 500 yards climb some stone steps on your right and then walk left through the wood to cross a low stile. Go right up a hill and then left onto a stunning balcony path along Cracker Edge with views over Dewsbury and the Pennines beyond. Follow this path round until it emerges onto Kirkgate with the Fox and Hounds public house on your right.

Do not turn oblique left down Kirkgate but walk straight ahead on Kirkgate and at No.15, on the left, go down steps and a narrow path to arrive at High Street. Cross over, turn right and then at Croft House go down stone steps to a path that passes between fields and factories. Emerge onto Grange Road, go straight across and follow a path over two stiles and up a set of stone steps

Cracker Edge at Dewsbury

onto a track. Follow this for 100 yards to reach Oaks Road. Turn left but after Oaks Cottage, on your left, do not follow Oaks Road round to the left but take the path straight ahead which leads into Bridle Street. Walk down to Soothill Lane, cross over, turn left and then first right again down Grace Leather Lane. Follow this as it bears left past some shops, on your left, and eventually comes to Broomsdale Road. Turn right and walk down Broomsdale Road to Lady Ann Road. Turn right and walk past Sykes Road, on your right. When Lady Ann Road turns sharp right do not follow it but go straight ahead on a gravel road past a workshop on your right and stables on your left. Just after the stables do not follow the track round to the right but walk straight ahead onto a narrow path. Follow this path until it meets another path and then turn right to walk under a railway bridge which also accommodates a stream behind a wall. You have now joined the Leeds Country Way which will be your companion for the next 22 miles. Walk up the tarmac road (Howley Mill Lane) to meet Timothy Lane, the B6123, at Batley.

BATLEY TO APPERLEY BRIDGE
11.5 miles

Walking from Birkby Brow Wood

Turn right and then almost immediately left up a path. After one third of a mile cross a wooden footbridge over a stream and continue straight ahead into Birkby Brow Wood. After a further third of a mile do not continue forward on the wide track but take a narrower but well defined track up to the right of the wood. Now stay to the right of the wood as it eventually bears right and the path emerges into a field.

Walk down the left of the field with the hedge on your left. At the end of the hedge turn left onto a lane (this is actually another section of Howley Mill Lane) and walk up to arrive at the A643 next to some cottages on your right.

Turn right and walk up the A643 to the traffic lights. Turn left and walk up the A650. Before you reach the roundabout cross over to the right of the A650 and then at the roundabout bear right to a pelican crossing over the A62. Cross this and then go right not up the A62 but up Street Lane.

Walk up Street Lane to No. 51 and turn left up Woodhead Road. Walk past the houses up a dirt track and after 300 yards take the path between the railings and the

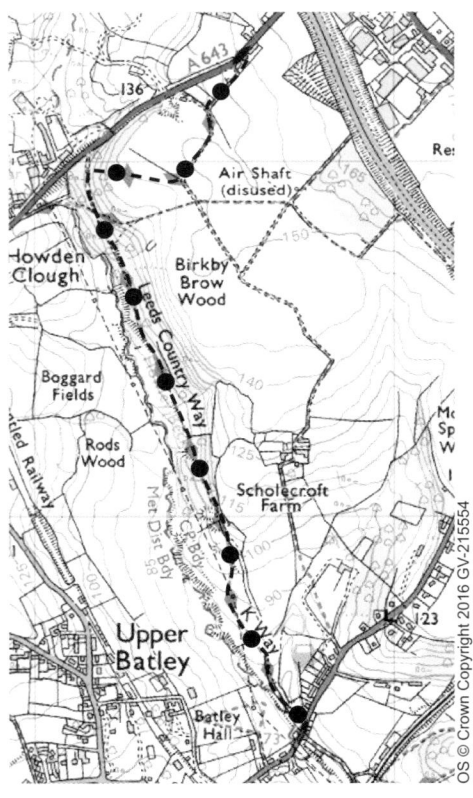

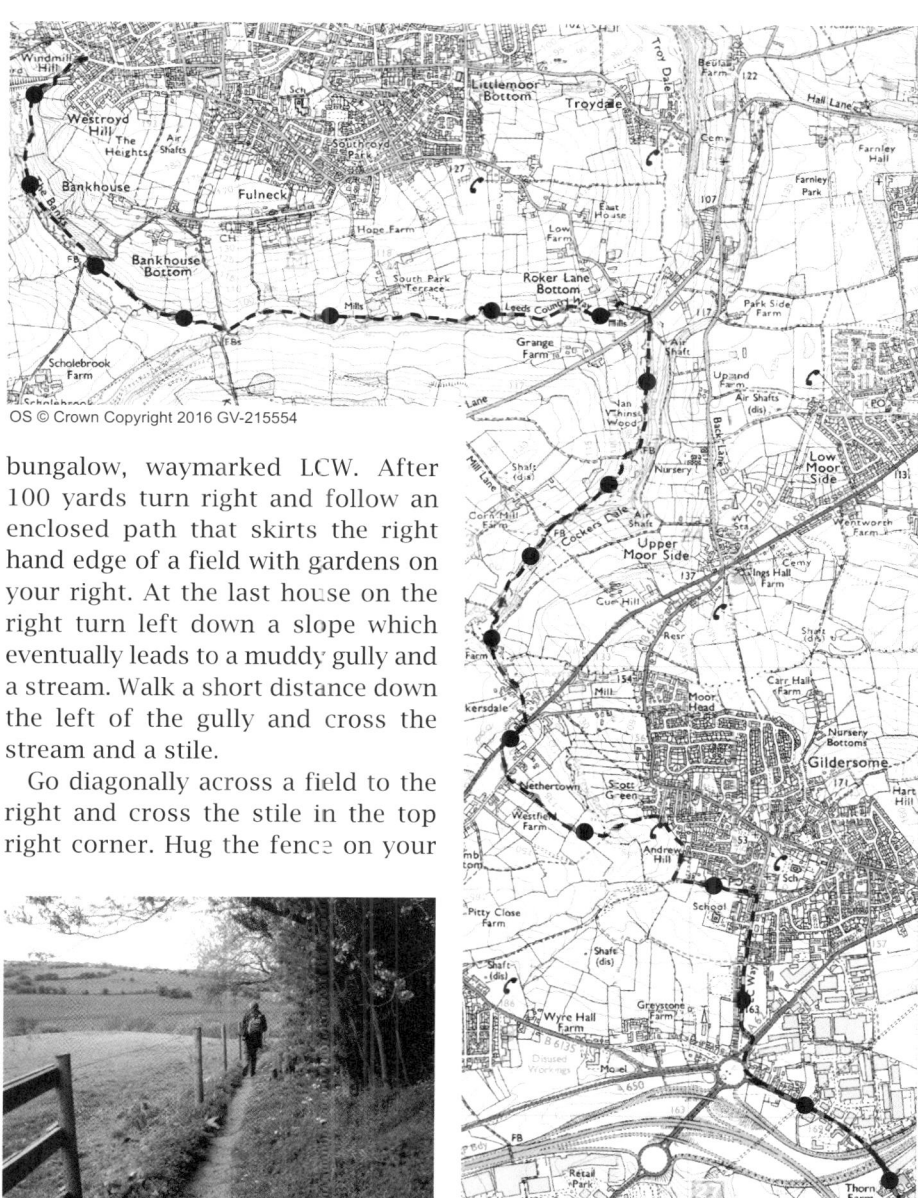
OS © Crown Copyright 2016 GV-215554

bungalow, waymarked LCW. After 100 yards turn right and follow an enclosed path that skirts the right hand edge of a field with gardens on your right. At the last house on the right turn left down a slope which eventually leads to a muddy gully and a stream. Walk a short distance down the left of the gully and cross the stream and a stile.

Go diagonally across a field to the right and cross the stile in the top right corner. Hug the fence on your

The path at Gildersome

right for 200 yards and then go over a stile on your right. Now keep close the fence on your left and walk up to the metal gate, past Shay Farm and into Old Lane.

Turn right and then immediately left down an enclosed path to the A58. Cross the road and walk up to the Valley Inn. Turn left and walk down to the bottom of Dale Road. Do not take the public footpath straight on but go right along the public bridleway, round a bend and bear right through a stile with the beck now on your right. Take a lovely walk with the beck on your right, ignoring all bridges on your right, until you eventually cross a field and a wooden bridge over the beck. On emerging into a wooded area do not turn right but take the path straight ahead up the bank. At the top of the bank turn left over a wooden bridge and follow this delightful elevated woodland path down to Tong Lane. Cross over and go down Roker Lane into Pudsey. After 160 yards turn left down a gillet and through a wooden stile. Now walk a ½ mile with the beck on your left and eventually down the left side of a golf course.

The beck at Pudsey

Halfway down the golf course you come to a three-way split. Do not take the metal bridge on your right or the concrete bridge straight ahead but bear half right onto a narrow path with a small beck on your right between you and the next part of the golf course. Eventually cross a field to a stile. Do not go left over a metal bridge but turn right and then left to continue your walk through the woods with the beck on your left. After ½ a mile the bridleway on the left bank comes over the beck to join you and you go right to follow the wide bridleway up the bank leaving the beck behind you.

At the top cross the bridge over the disused railway line and walk up to Smalewell Road. Turn left and walk past the Fox and Grapes pub. Take the next left and walk down to the end of the road. At the bottom do not go straight on to Delph End but bear right down the bridleway to Gibraltar Road. After 200 yards a private road joins from the right but continue in the same direction. After a further 200 yards meet another road but still continue in the same direction up to 'Pudsey Marble and Granite' on your left. Go left in front of this and take the public bridleway signed Wild Grove.

Follow the cobbled path up the hill which eventually bears left and becomes a stony path between trees. Turn right at the waymarked sign 'Pudsey Link and Leeds Country Way', go between buildings and walk down to the railway crossing. Cross with care and walk up Daleside Road, past Thornbury Cricket ground on your right and up to the A647. Turn right and cross at the pelican crossing.

Walk along until you are opposite the shops and then go left up a fenced path with a cricket ground on your left. At the top right hand corner turn left along an overgrown track with the cricket ground still on your left. At the top left hand corner go straight ahead to emerge onto a wide woodland track and turn right.

After 100 yards go between two wooden fences and immediately left over a stone stile to cross diagonally right across two fields. At the other side go over a stile and bear right to join an enclosed path leading onto a golf course. Walk across the golf course,

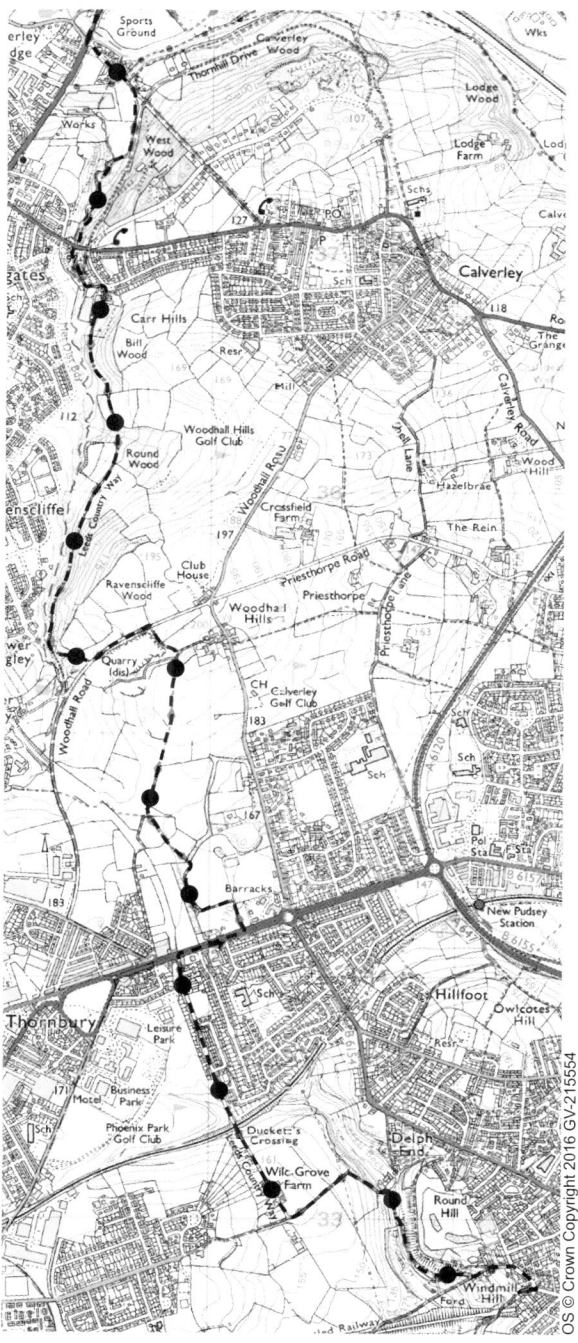

67

crossing several fairways to a wooden gate on the other side. 80 yards beyond the gate turn left down a track waymarked 'Leeds Country Way' with a quarry on your left.

Come to a T-junction and turn left down a wide track to the bottom. Before the Blue Pig pub, and just after the Lodge House, turn obliquely right and follow this path for a mile ignoring numerous paths to the left and right. Eventually pass Francis Willy British Wools Mill on your right and reach Crowther Lane.

Pass the mill entrance and the Lodge and go left down a path waymarked 'Calverley mm Way'. Go over the beck and turn right. Cross a stile by a ford and bear left up the cobbled lane to cross the A657. Pass through an opening between a stone post and a wall to the right of Carbottom Road and follow the downhill path into the wooded area. Follow this path through Westwood for ¼ of a mile before bearing right uphill to a broad track. Turn left and walk down to the bottom, over the canal and up to the A658.

Do not cross the A658 but turn right onto Apperley Bridge.

Crossing the canal at Apperley

BRIAN CLOUGH AT LEEDS

Surprisingly, Brian became manager of Leeds United in 1974 after openly criticising the team and the previous manager, Don Revie (see 'Brian Clough at Middlesbrough'). He was sacked acrimoniously after 44 days.

Unsurprisingly the walk circumnavigates Leeds.

Elland Road, Leeds

For those wishing to visit the Elland Road Stadium: Before Gildersome, at the point where you walk up the A643 to the traffic lights, do not turn right but continue straight on to a bus stop on the left. Numerous buses will take you the three miles to the stadium.

APPERLEY BRIDGE TO HAREWOOD
12.3 miles

Cross Appleby Bridge over the River Aire, walking down to the entrance to the sports fields on your right. Turn right and walk down the enclosed path between two roads. This eventually goes right towards the river and then left with the river immediately on your right.

After ¾ of a mile the path bears right away from the river on an enclosed path to the left of a field. Go through a stile at the far end and turn obliquely left up a road to a T-junction at a dirt track.

Turn right and walk up to Woodlands Drive. Turn right and on entering a private road turn left and ascend a walled path with superb views of the Aire Valley to your left. At the top, turn left and walk to the end of New York Lane. Turn left and walk the short distance to the A65.

The River Aire

Cross the A65 at the pelican crossing and go right for 100 yards before turning left at the public footpath sign and descend into a field. Cross diagonally right to the next stile and ascend the steps passing behind a house

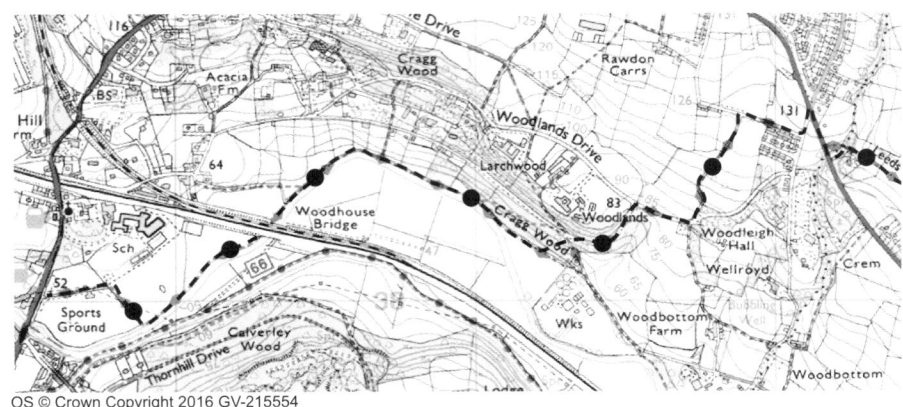

OS © Crown Copyright 2016 GV-215554

into a hedge lined path. Go over a stile into a field and walk towards the left corner to cross into an enclosed track. Go over another wooden stile and walk up the left side of a field.

Emerge into a lane but go straight across into another enclosed path. Pass through the side of a gate and continue between houses to West End Grove. Turn left and walk 200 yards up the road before turning right into West End Lane. Immediately after the school turn left up a public footpath between the school and houses and cross a wooden bridge into a wood. Follow the path that bears left and at the top of the wood turn right along a broader path through the wood with the boundary fence on your left.

Follow this through the wood to a kissing gate and walk down the left edge of a field to go over a stile into Lee Lane (a dirt track). Turn left and just before reaching houses and a road turn right towards the college playing fields. Just before reaching the playing fields, turn left and then immediately right down a hedged path to Brownberry Lane.

Cross over and immediately go left over a stone stile into a wood. Go through a metal kissing gate in the middle of the wood. At the far side do not go left over a stile but take the path right through the wood with the boundary fence on your left. When the boundary fence on your left finishes you continue straight ahead through the middle of the wood to a stile.

Emerge into a field keeping the hedge on your right and on arriving at a wall turn right with the wall now on your left. Cross three stiles and then walk to the right of the Leeds Bradford Airport landing lights before going over a stile on your left at the end of the wall. Turn right down the Water Authority road to Scotland Lane.

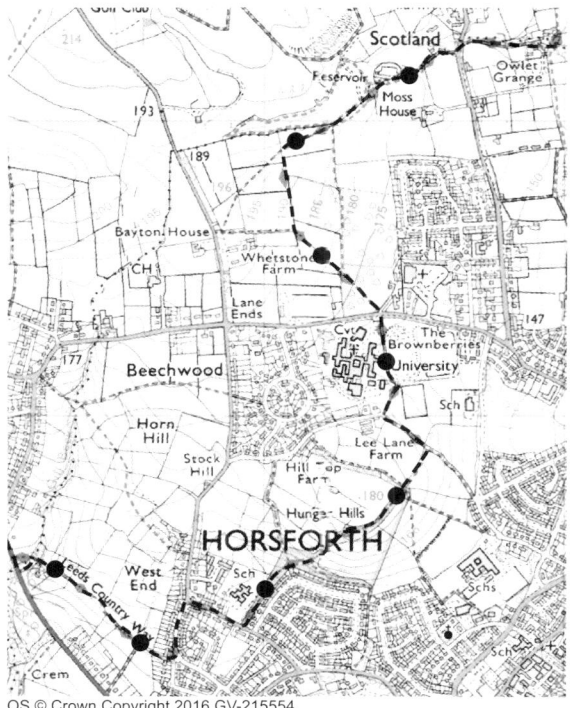

Cross the lane and turn left down the access road to Owlet Farm. Just after Owlet Grange and before Owlet Cottage, turn right to pass between the properties, over a stone stile and into a field. Turn left and skirt the right hand side of a horse arena. Go through a kissing gate and walk up the left of a field. Go through the gate and gap stile and across the middle of the next field. Go over a stile and walk down the right of the next field before bearing right across a small grassy area to a stile in the bottom right hand corner. Descend the steps into the lane, turn right and walk down to the railway bridge.

Cross the railway bridge and walk up the lane opposite. Follow this lane for ¼ of a mile to a cricket ground on your right where you turn right and walk down the right of the ground before turning left and walking along the top. On arriving at the top left hand corner of the cricket ground go down a public footpath behind houses.

The path eventually emerges onto Cookridge Lane. Turn right and after a ¼ of a mile turn left into Pinfold Lane. Pass Rushes Farm on your left before the lane becomes a stony track. The track eventually turns right to Old Rushes

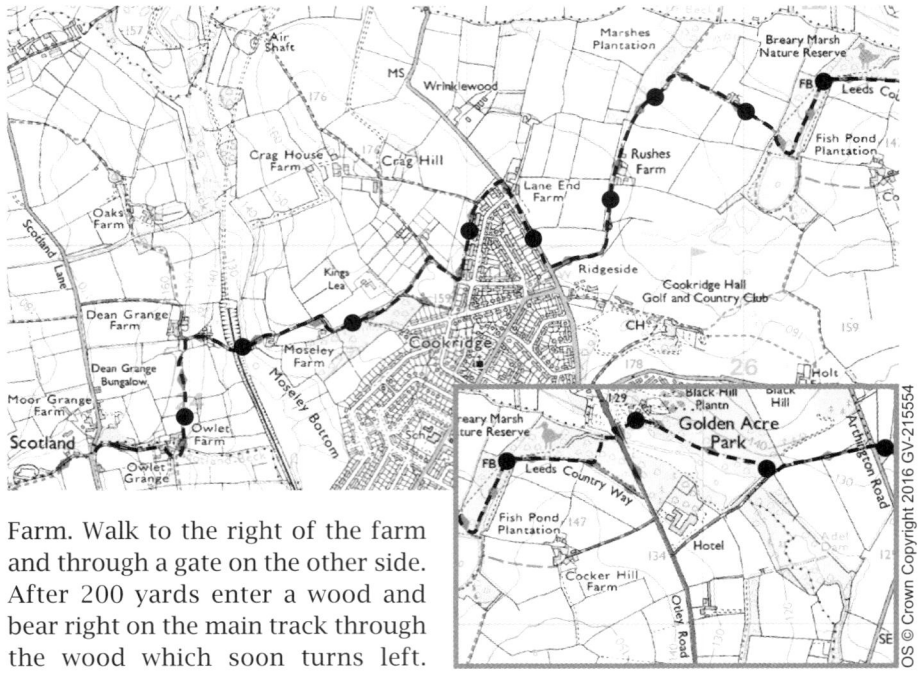

Farm. Walk to the right of the farm and through a gate on the other side. After 200 yards enter a wood and bear right on the main track through the wood which soon turns left.

Follow the path but just before reaching Otley Road, the A60, turn left along a board walk. At the end of the board walk turn right to go through a tunnel under the A60 and into Golden Acre Park.

Once in the park turn right and walk round the right hand side of the park and the lake. On crossing a bridge at the top of the lake bear half right onto a path waymarked the 'Meewood Valley trail' (do not walk up to the car park)

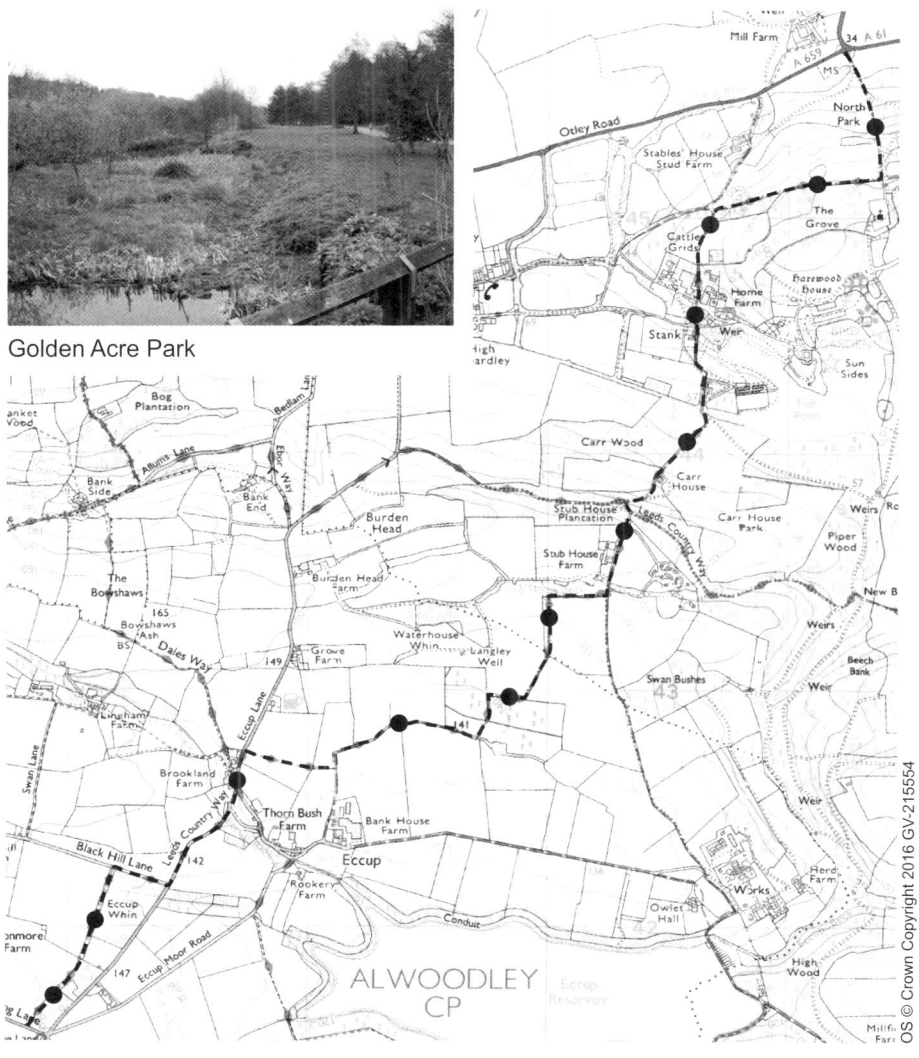

Golden Acre Park

and come to Arthington Road. Go straight across into King Lane and walk 400 yards before turning left over a stile and into a wood. Follow this main path through the wood which eventually bears right to Blackfield Lane.

Turn right and walk 300 yards to the T-junction. Turn left up Ecup Lane for ½ a mile, passing Brookland farm on your left. 200 yards after Brookland Farm go right over a stile and walk across the middle of a field on a broad track. Go over a stile and cross another field keeping the hedge on your right. Go over another wooden stile and turn left onto a bridleway.

Follow this clearly marked bridleway as it meanders its way past plantations and through fields across the beautiful Harewood Estate. Be sure to notice Emmerdale (the location for the TV series) on your right. Pass the second entrance into Emmerdale and drop down into a wood. Come to a four way junction. It is here that we leave the Leeds Country Way. Go straight across and follow the path down to the left. This then bears right and meets a broad track. Turn right and after 100 yards the track bears left at a waymarker telling you are on the Ebor Way. At the bottom of the hill enjoy the view of the lake and Harewood House.

Bear left through a gate and up the hill. Walk down to a crossroads with a bridge on your right and one straight ahead. Cross the bridge straight ahead and walk up a steep hill past the Harewood Estate Office on your right and emerge over a cattle grid onto a concrete road. At the end of the concrete road come to

Harewood House and lake

four-way junction. Take an oblique right up a hill and when the road flattens out, and after a further 300 yards, take a grassy public footpath down to the left. Follow this down the hill, through the drive of a house and out onto the junction of the A61 and A659.

HAREWOOD TO KNARESBOROUGH
9.7 miles

Walk north up the A61 and cross the road bridge over the river. 100 yards past the bridge turn right down Bridge Court and eventually onto a path with the river on your right. After about ½ a mile do not take the path on the left across the middle of a field but continue on the path next to the river (this can be very overgrown).

The River Wharfe Near Harewood Bridge

Come to a point where the path ahead appears to run out but continue back on yourself round the right hand edge of the field until you come to a wooden bridge on your right. Cross over and turn right to follow the right edge of the field next to the river.

At the top right hand corner of this very long field leave the river and cross a metal bridge on your left over a beck. Turn right and walk up between trees, up a bank and between farm buildings to a road. Cross over to the stile opposite and walk up a long narrow field to the top right corner where you emerge onto a road. Walk left along the road for 150 yards and take the road right to Barrowby. This is Moor Lane.

At the triangular junction at the top turn left and after 100 yards turn right down a bridleway called Lund Head Lane with a stone wall on your right. Walk past a farm on your right, onto a grassy path and through a gate onto Marsh Lane.

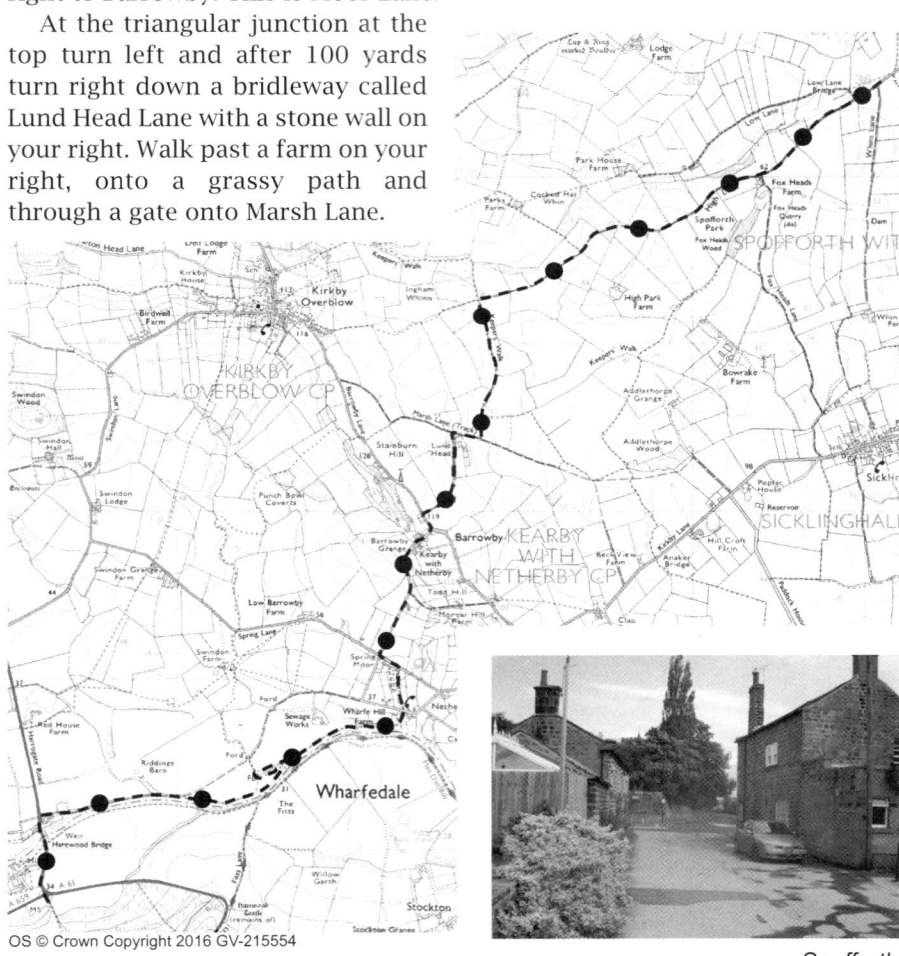

Spofforth

Turn right down this stony path between fields and at the bottom of the hill pass through a metal gate stile on your left. You are now on Keepers Walk and it passes along the left hand side of several fields. On reaching a gate leading into a copse on your left turn right and walk down the right hand side of three fields. At the top right hand corner of the third field do not take the track to the left but continue straight ahead on a farm track. After ½ a mile do not take the public bridleway right but continue on the dirt track road straight ahead.

This track eventually becomes a country lane and after 200 yards turn left through a gate and diagonally across a field with Spofforth cricket ground on your left. At the far side walk under the railway bridge and then straight on through a wooden gate. Pass between buildings into the village of Spofforth. Walk straight ahead down the A66 past White Horse Mews and the church. After a further 100 yards turn left down the public footpath with the River Crimple on your left.

Keep this river on your left while walking through five fields. Eventually cross a stile and where one path continues straight ahead next to the river take a right hand path up the right side of a field to the top right hand corner. Pass between trees and emerge to walk up the right hand side of a large field towards the A66.

Emerge onto the A66, cross the road and walk right, up the hill until you turn left towards Locksley Farm Barns on a public bridleway. Walk through the gates between West Lodge and East Lodge and follow the road to where it splits. Take the road left and almost immediately through a gate on your left. Cross a field to

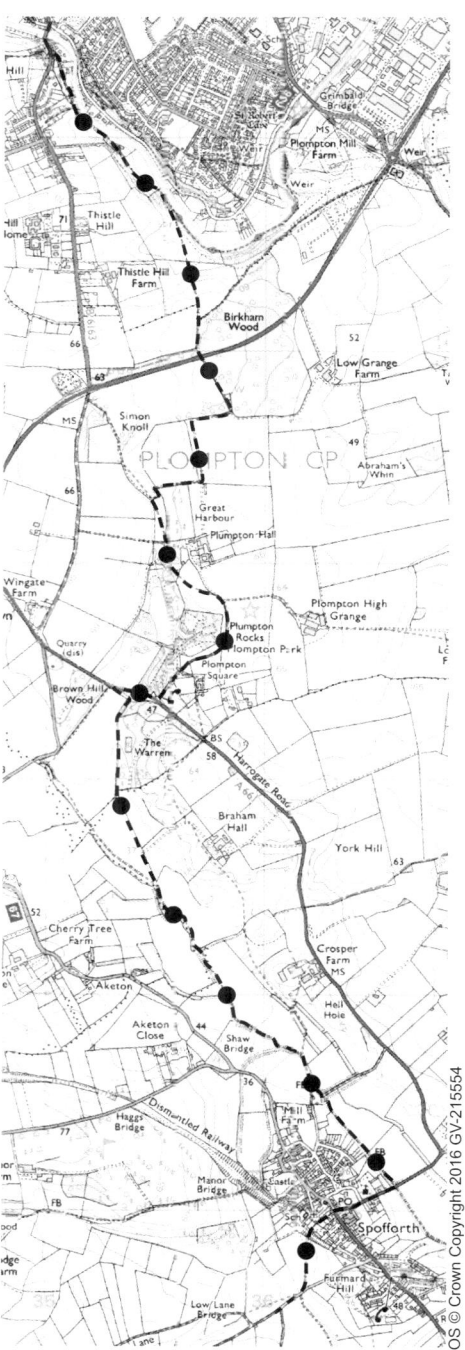

77

the top left corner and pass through a wooden gate onto a grassy path through woodland.

On reaching a farm track turn left and then right to skirt a wood on your right. After 400 yards the path turns right, then left and then right, round the edge of the wood. On clearing the edge of the wood, emerge onto a track with Plumpton Hall on your right. Turn left and walk up the left hand side of a field with the hall directly behind you before bearing right to a waymarked path off to your left. This narrow path skirts a wood on the right and eventually crosses the A658, continuing in the same direction.

After 200 yards take the left fork away from the wood and over a stile into the left hand corner of a field. Walk down this field with Knaresborough church on the horizon. At the bottom of the hill pass through a wooden kissing gate and walk across the next field towards woodland. Pass through another kissing gate and walk the short distance through the woodland down to the River Nidd.

Turn left and walk with the river on your right before the path leaves the river briefly to pass through the middle of fields. Emerge out onto a track

Knaresborough

with a house on your right. The path passes to the left of a fence before rejoining the river. Continue on the path through the woods ignoring any paths going to the left. On reaching a wall do not take the left path to Calcut but continue straight on, signposted to Knaresborough and low bridge. Eventually emerge onto a road and continue in the same direction. Reach the B6163 and cross the road to go right, past the Dropping Well Inn and over the river and into Knaresborough.

KNARESBOROUGH TO BOROUGHBRIDGE
9.4 miles

Take the first left down Waterside. Continue on this road with the river on your left and eventually climb Gallons Steps on your right next to the old Dye House. At the top of the steps cross the road and walk up Hilton Lane with the railway station on your left. On reaching High Street walk straight across and up Raw Gap. On reaching Stockwell Road turn left over the railway bridge and then immediately right to follow the public footpath. Pass allotments on your left.

When the path turns left between the allotments continue straight ahead with the railway line on your right. Emerge on to a road and walk straight on with buildings on your right until you meet a main road. Cross over, go right and then left into an un-named road with the

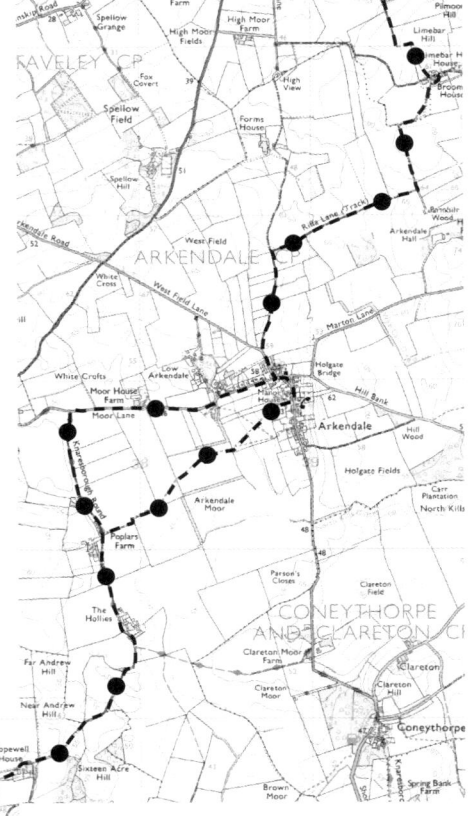

public footpath sign on the corner. Bear left down Half Crown Way to Sterling Chase and continue straight down past Guinea Croft on your left to cross a stile at the bottom of the road. Emerge into a large field and make towards the top left hand corner.

Cross into a narrow country lane and turn right before going over a stile on the left into an even bigger field. Make your way towards an electricity pylon on the far side of the field with a reservoir on your right. At the other side of the field go over a stile to the right of a gate and walk up through woodland to a road. Turn right and the bear immediately left down a dirt road. Just before reaching Knaresborough Golf Club, on your left, pass through a waymarked gate on your right. Follow this path to farm buildings on your right at Hopewell House. Do not turn right towards the house but continue straight ahead up a bank and along the farm track. Stay on this well established farm track and on reaching The Hollies Farm the path goes directly through the farm and out of the other side. At this point you are joining the Knaresborough Round for just one mile.

Pass Poplar cottage on your left and walk on to a T-junction. There turn right and walk along the road to Arkendale.

Arkendale

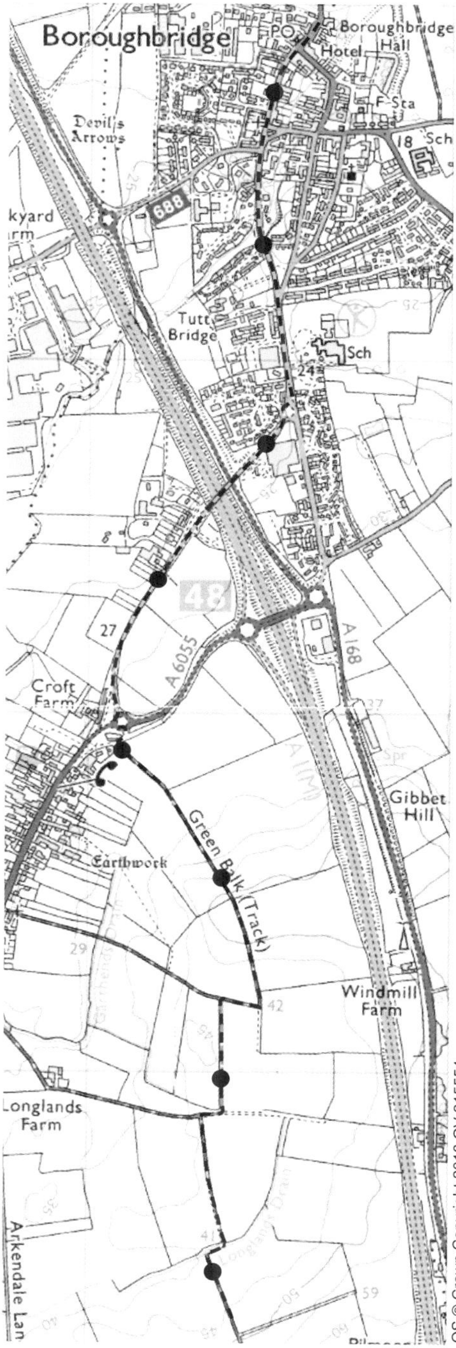

On reaching The Blue Bell go left down Westfield Lane.

When the road bears left just after Sunnyside Farm take the bridle path almost straight ahead. After a ¼ mile the bridle path turns sharp right. At the crest of the hill, when the bridleway turns right, turn left down the right hand side of a field. At the top right corner of the field turn right for 150 yards and then left towards Lime Bar Hill House Farm. Make sure you go to the left of all the farm buildings and follow a track up the right hand side of a field. Where the hedge on your right ends zigzag left and then right and continue in the same direction.

This emerges onto a hardcore farm track which goes to the bottom of the hill, zigzags and climbs slightly still heading north with the sometimes noisy A1 on your right. On arriving at a T-junction turn right and walk towards the A1. After 30 yards turn left and walk up the left hand side of a field. At the top left corner pass through the hedge and turn right onto a wide bridleway. After 100 yards just follow the grass track round to the left. This track is called The Green Balk Track. Pass Green Balk Farm on your left and walk across the grass to the A6055.

Cross over, turn right and take the path to the left of the road island, emerging onto the pavement on the left of a minor road leading into Boroughbridge. Cross over the A1 and down to a road island. Take the second exit and walk down into Boroughbridge.

Boroughbridge

BOROUGHBRIDGE TO THIRSK
11.5 miles

Walk past the Crown Hotel, over the River Ure and turn right down a public footpath with the river on your right. Walk for approximately a ¼ mile to Milby Lock and cross left over the footbridge. Walk with the river on your right for 50 yards before the path turns left between hedges up to a wooden gate. Cross the stile on the right and follow Tinkler Lane round to the right to meet Moor Lane at a T-junction.

Turn right and walk 3 miles to Thornton Bridge, passing Burton Grange Farm and Treble Sykes Farm, with views of the White Horse on the Cleveland Hills ahead of you. Warning! This is easy walking on a quiet road but traffic does come on to you quickly so walk on the right hand side and always step onto the grass verge when traffic approaches.

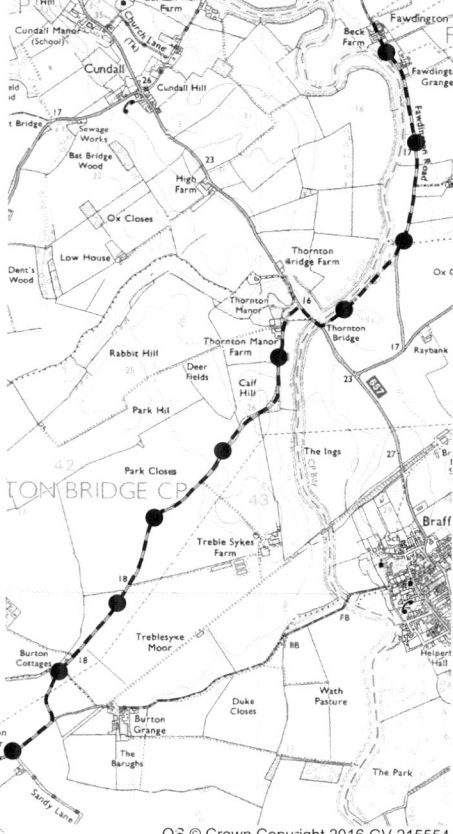

OS © Crown Copyright 2016 GV-215554

On arriving at the T-junction at Thornton Bridge turn right and cross the bridge over the River Swale. Once over the bridge go left on a public footpath with the river now on your left until it meets Fawdington Road. Turn left and walk in a northerly direction past Fawdington House, Fawdington Grange before passing Beck Farm on your left and going straight ahead onto a rough farm track. When the track goes right, almost immediately continue straight ahead on a more grassy track.

Walk past Crow Wood on your right and eventually cross a beck between fences and up to a T-junction at a track. Turn right and after 100 yards take the public footpath on the left. On reaching Oxclose Lane turn right and then immediately left to pick up the public bridleway up the left hand side of a field climbing up Eldmire Hill. Then walk down the other side of the hill to pass through a gap in a hedge and follow a path down the left hand side of a field.

The River Swale from Thornton Bridge

Emerge onto a tarmac road in Dalton and walk to a T-junction. Turn right and at the end of Pittings Lane turn left. After 200 yards at the give way sign go right, which is almost straight on. Walk round to

Dalton

the next T-junction and turn left signposted Sowerby and Thirsk. Walk about ¼ of a mile and on a bend go left into Paradise Farm (a sign says 'Private, Paradise Farm only' but it's alright). Walk up the drive for 100 yards and at the first bend the path goes straight on through the hedge. Walk behind some wooden sheds to a grassed area and find a wooden footbridge in the left hand corner. Cross the footbridge and proceed up the middle of a corn field. Walk through the hedge and across the middle of the next field towards two trees. Walk between the trees and proceed to the left of Dalton Cottage Farm.

Walk to the left and behind the farm buildings and emerge into a rough meadow area with a beck on your left. It may be quite obscure but in the middle of the hedge opposite is a wooden gate and bridge over the beck. On the other side you may encounter one of the toughest parts of your walk so far. The area is very overgrown but you need to go right and make your way to the bridge under the railway line by keeping close to the beck on your right. Walk under the railway line and into a field and walk

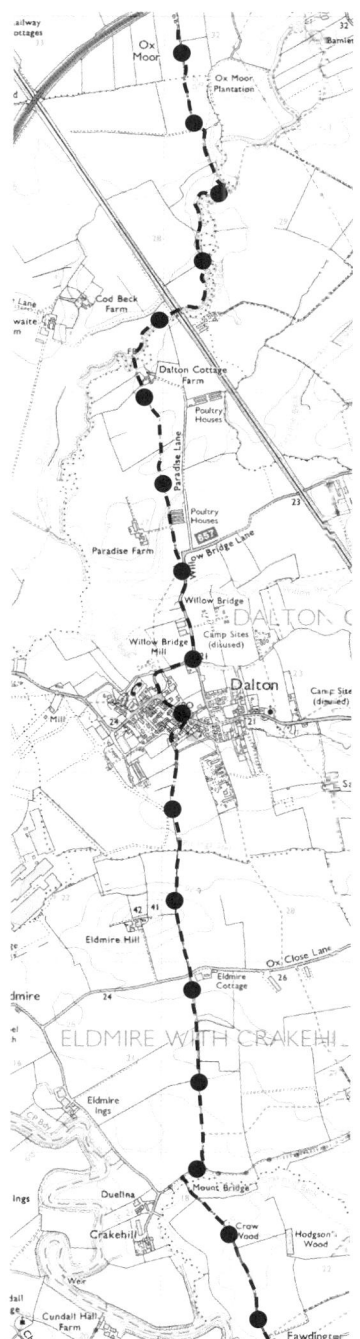

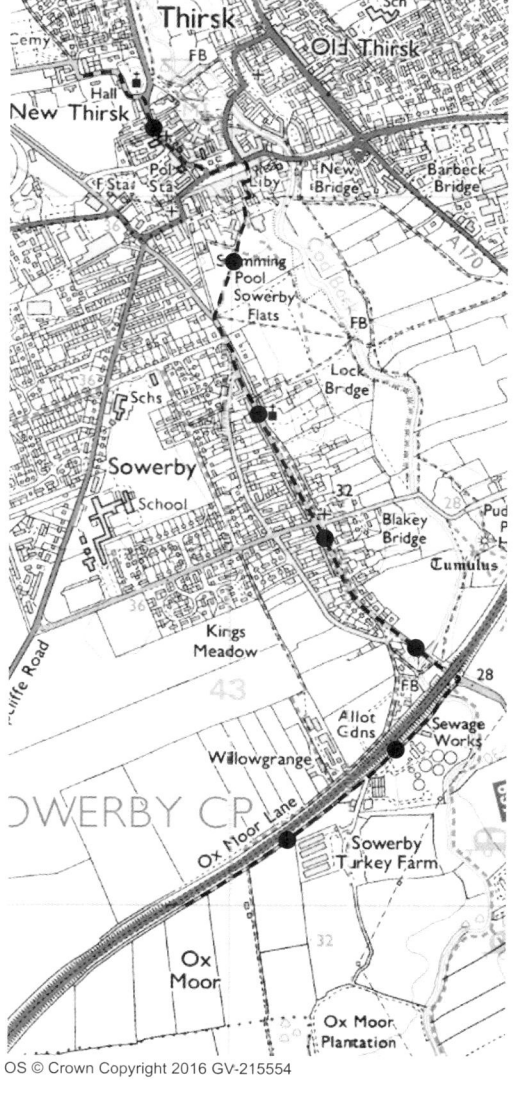

OS © Crown Copyright 2016 GV-215554

diagonally to the far left hand corner to exit between metal railings. Follow the path round for about 100 yards and then pass through a waymarked metal gate.

Now simply walk with the fence and the beck on your immediate right for as far as you can go. Then look for a waymarked stile about 30 yards to the left of the beck in the middle of a hedge. Go over the stile and walk up the right hand side of the next field past a wood to join a gravel track heading towards the A168 in the distance.

On arriving at the A168 turn right over a stile and walk down a lane with the A168 on your immediate left. Join Sandholmes Lane at the sewage works and continue in the same direction to a T-junction. At the T-junction walk left under the A168 and up into Sowerby. Pass Blakey Lane and the church on your right and opposite Holyrood House, on the left, take the path diagonally across the Sports recreation area on your right. Eventually walk down an alleyway between a brick wall and some cottages. Cross straight over Chapel Street and up a cobbled public way through into Thirsk market place.

Thirsk market place

THIRSK TO BROMPTON
12 miles

Leave Thirsk Market Place by walking up Kirkgate and just before St Mary's Church go left into Cemetery Road. After a couple of bends turn right into Westlands Lane. Continue with the back of houses on your right and eventually emerge onto a grassy track.

After ¼ of a mile the path passes through the middle of a corn field with the beautiful Cleveland hills over to your right. Pass through a gate and go diagonally across to the top left hand corner of the next field and through another gate. The path now swings left with the hedge on your right. After a few hundred yards cross a track but keep going in a northerly direction and pass a seat with the inscription 'Barnaby' on it.

After a further ¼ of a mile, at the corner of a field, do not go straight on but bear left with a hedge still on your right. After 100 yards the path goes between the hedge to the right and climbs a hill with excellent views of the Vale of Mowbray to your left. At the top of the hill the path bears left and skirts Big Wood. Half way down the wood look carefully for a path entering the wood on the right and passing over a waymarked wooden bridge. Emerge onto a narrow path with a fence on your left and trees on your right. This leads into Thornton le Street Stud. Make your way towards the stud buildings straight ahead.

Pass to the right of the stud and head for the middle of the trees defining the boundary on the far side. Walk between the trees and across the middle of the next field to a six-bar metal gate. Make a short climb to a rusty metal gate and then on in a northerly direction. When the main track turns left go straight ahead and skirt the grounds of Beal House on your right.

On clearing the grounds on your right continue straight ahead down

Thornton le Street Stud

the right hand side of a field with a hedge of trees on your right. This path can get quite overgrown, so persevere! When the hedge runs out on your right

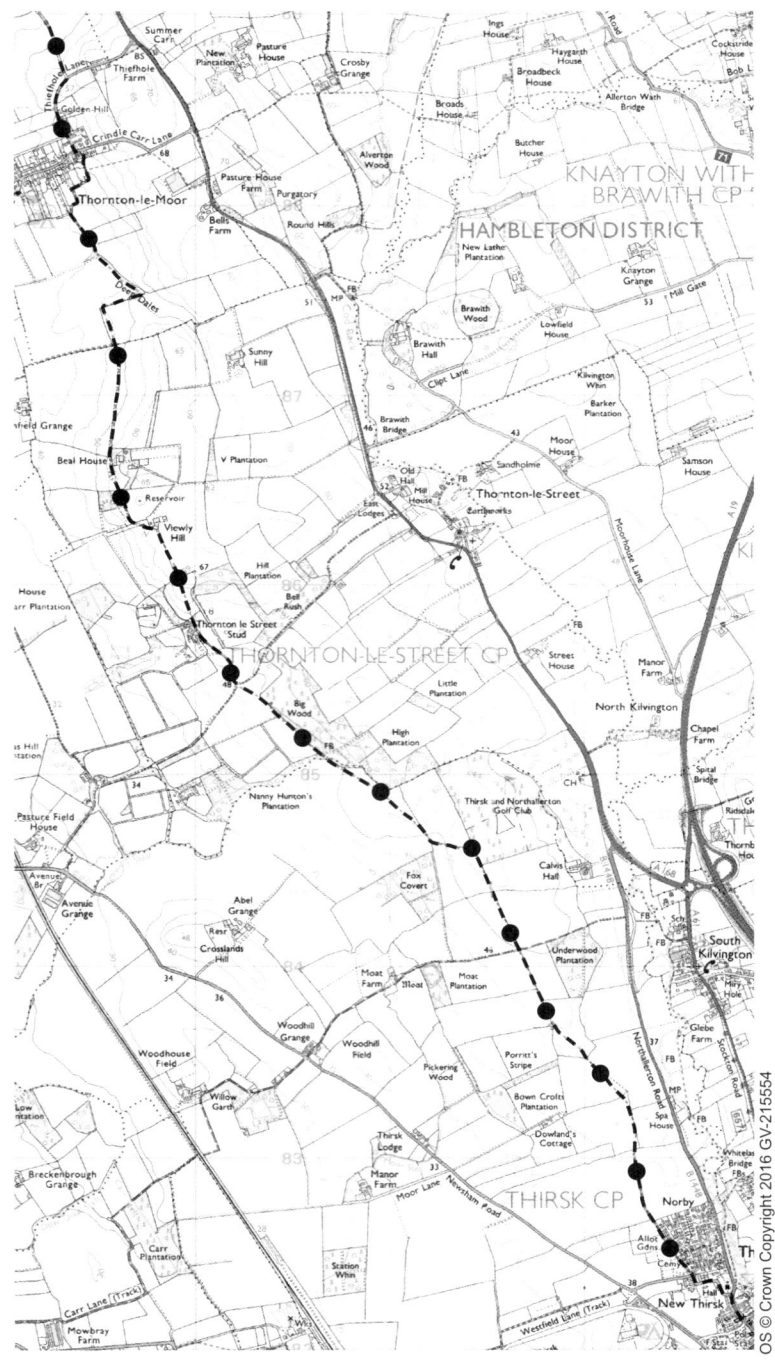

continue down the left hand side of the next field with the hedge on your left and cross over a stile. Turn right and walk 200 yards down to a wooden footbridge before going left up a grassy path between hedges. Follow this path up into Thornton le Moor.

On reaching the road turn left and then immediately right up Thiefhold Lane. Walk past the bus stop and the road climbs round to the right. After about 300 yards turn left down a track. On reaching a T-junction at Brockholme Farm turn right and walk a short distance to the A168. Walk left along the A168 for about 200 yards before turning left into a track signposted to Thornborough Farm.

Follow the track round to the farm and at the far end of the farmyard bear slightly right through a six-bar metal gate. Walk down the left of a field and at the top left corner go through another gate. Turn left and walk up a rough path with the hedge on your left. Cross a track and walk diagonally down

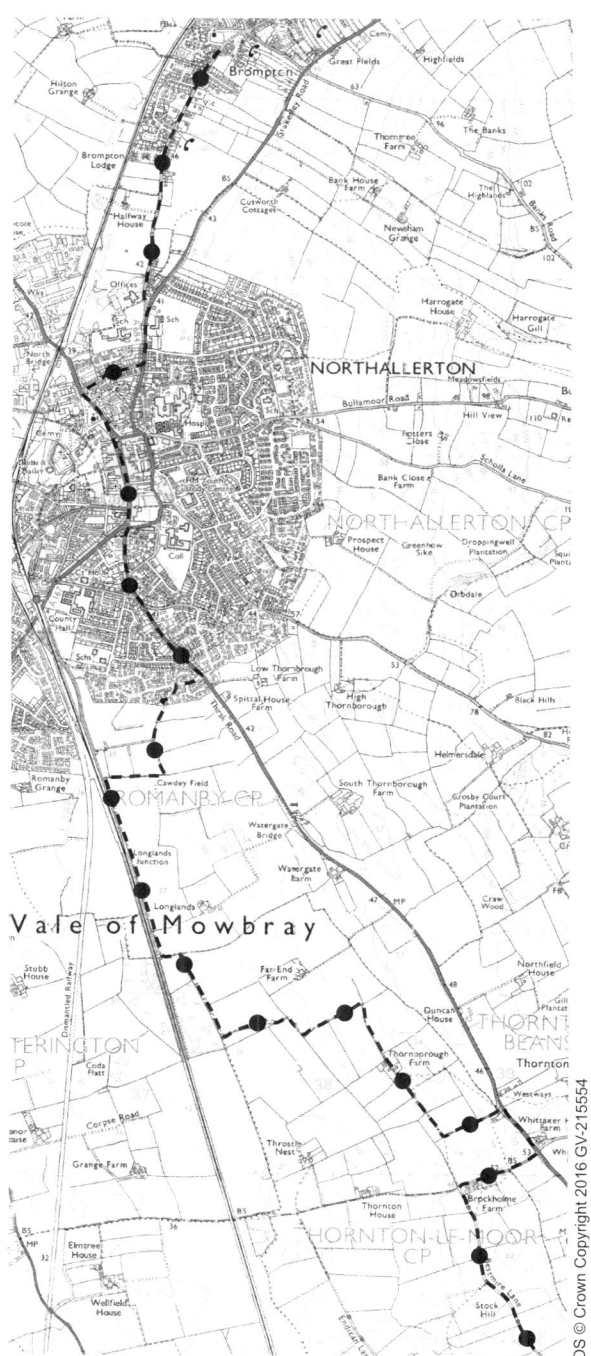

89

the middle of a field to an open gate. Pass through the gate and walk down the left of a field towards a wood. At the bottom left hand corner turn right and walk north with the wood on your left. Once again this path can be very uneven and overgrown.

When the wood ends keep the hedge on your left and walk towards a stile in the left hand corner of the field. Climb over the stile and proceed left. On arriving at the railway line turn right and walk for about a mile with the railway on your left.

Looking towards Thornton Le Moor

Cross over a stile and turn right. Go through a metal gate and carry straight on in an easterly direction. Climb over a stile and continue with a fence on your right. At the bottom right hand corner of the field turn left and, keeping the fence and trees on your right, head in a northerly direction. Go over a stile through a six-bar gate and go right along the edge of a field to a stile in the right corner. Go over this style into a path with a hedge on one side and a fence on the other, cross over a wooden bridge and emerge into a cul de sac.

Northallerton

Walk right to the end of the cul de sac and turn left. Walk up to the end of St John's Close and turn right. Walk to the end of St James Drive before turning left onto the A168. Walk for ½ a mile to arrive in High Street in the middle of Northallerton.

Walk past the council offices on High Street over the roundabout and past the church before going right into Quaker Lane. At the top turn left past the school and at the mini roundabout bear left to Brompton. Walk up Northallerton Road and on arriving in Brompton proceed past the Church and green, on your left, to the crossroads. Walk straight across to the right of the Three Horse Shoes pub into Cockpit Hill.

BROMPTON TO YARM
13 miles

Every effort was made to follow paths to Yarm but the simple truth is that at the time of writing virtually all of the paths either don't exist anymore or are hopelessly overgrown. What proved a delightful surprise was that the alternative proved to be some of the best country lane walking you could possibly hope for.

Lanes that are virtually free of traffic and yet well maintained make for good progress. As this part of the walk is very flat this does facilitate walking even in wet weather.

Walk up Cockpit Hill and down the other side. Stay on the right of the green and the river and after 300 yards pass the Village Inn. Pass a bridge and a ford on your left and eventually bear right into Little Lane. Walk 150 yards up to a T-junction at the A684 and turn left. Stay on the pavement for ½ a mile and turn left into Long Lane signposted to Deighton and Wellbury. After 200 yards pass Hallikeld Farm on your right. After a further mile cross a railway line. After a further ½ a mile you cross Wainwright's Coast to Coast walk

Brompton

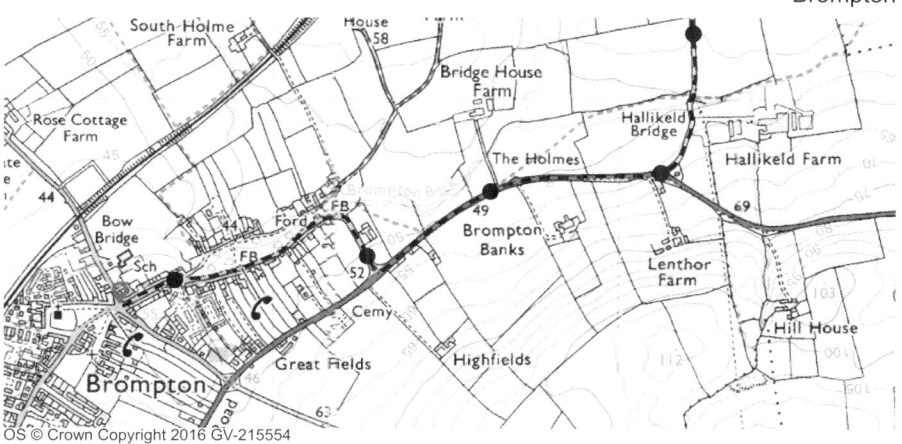

OS © Crown Copyright 2016 GV-215554

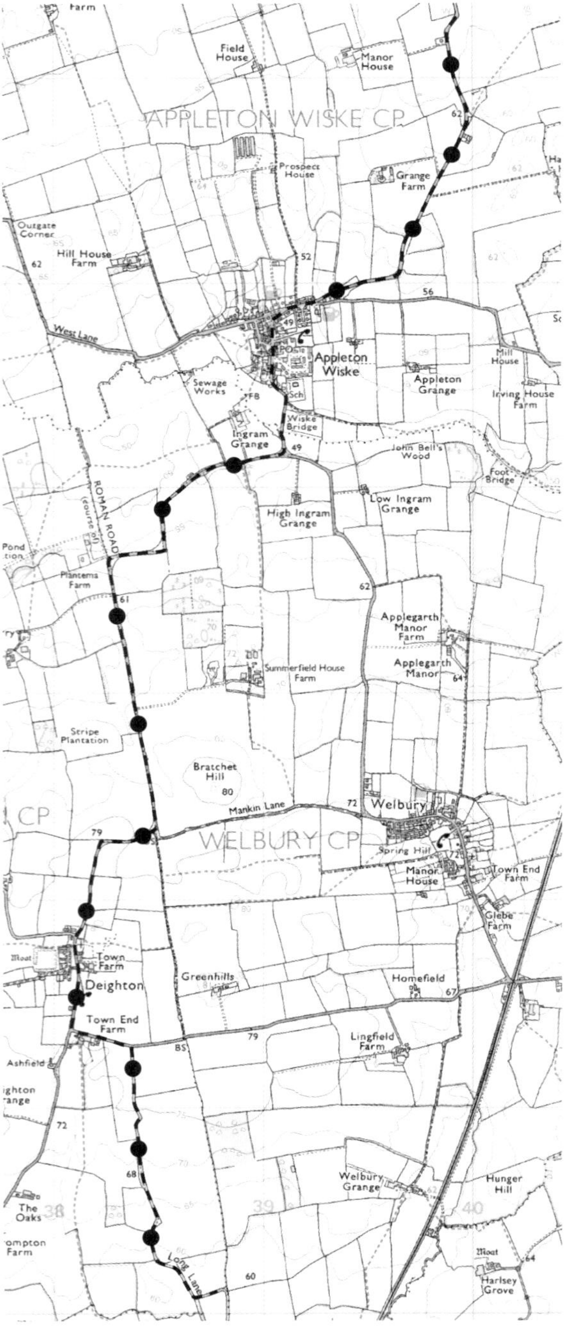

but continue heading north up Long Lane. After a further mile come to a T-junction signposted left to Deighton and Appleton Whiske. Turn left and after 300 yards turn right onto Deighton Lane. Follow the

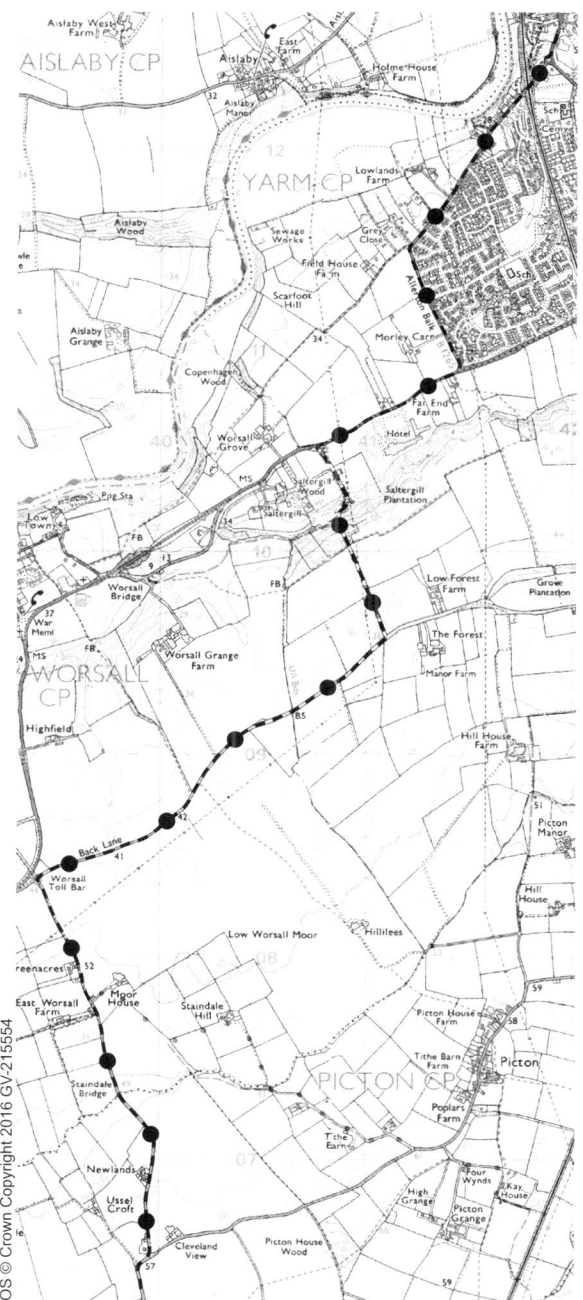

road north through the village of Deighton. After a mile pass Blackberry Farm on your left hand side and after another mile come to a T-junction on a bend. Turn left into the lovely village of Appleton Whiske by crossing a stream and walking up Front Street.

At the top of the village walk between houses and the pub to a T-junction. Turn right and on leaving the village take the left fork to Picton and Worsall. After a further mile take a road to the left on a bend signposted Worsall and Yarm. Walk past Swallowfields on your left hand side and after a mile, just before a T-junction, turn right into Back Lane.

After a mile pass Worsall Grange Farm on your left and then 400 yards later the 'Welcome to Stockton on Tees' sign. Walk another 400 yards and look for a farm track on the left (if you reach Low Forest Barns you have missed the track). Walk up the track, through a wood, and emerge into Saltergill Lane. Pass Saltergill Hall on your left and walk up to the B1264. Cross over with care and turn right.

93

Appleton Whiske

Pass Tall Trees Nursery on your right and after a further 600 yards turn left into Allerton Balk Lane, the B1265. Pass Everingham Road and Sefton Way on your right hand side before going under an arched railway bridge to a road island. Walk straight ahead down the A67 and into the delightful town of Yarm.

YARM TO MIDDLESBROUGH (TRANSPORTER BRIDGE)
11.5 miles

The River Tees at Yarm

Walk out of Yarm in a northerly direction and at the far end cross over the River Tees. Immediately follow the signs for the Teesdale Way by turning right and then right again in front of the Blue Bell pub to access the riverside path. Follow this path away from the bridge in an easterly direction. The Teesdale Way waymarker is a yellow disc with a black crow. After 400 yards you will see a white futuristic building on the other side of the river. Do not be deterred by any 'private fishing' signs as these are purely to discourage anglers and not walkers. The river quickly turns north and the path becomes very distinct while passing numerous fishing points.

After 1.8 miles do not go left to Eaglescliffe but continue on the path next to the river, sign posted 'golf club', until after 2 miles you cannot go any further. At this point the path turns away from the river and uphill with the golf course on your right. At the top of the hill the path turns a right angle to the right along the back of some houses. Emerge into Dinsdale Drive and walk forward for 300 yards before turning left up Carnoustie Drive. Pass The Links Primary School on your right and continue up Carnoustie Drive until you come to

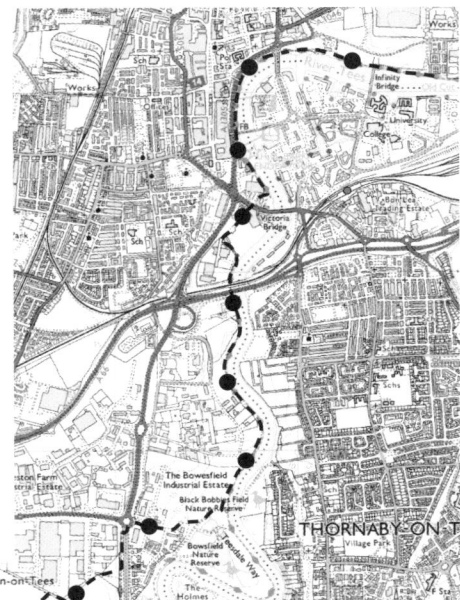

a T-junction at the A135. Walk along the pavement to your right for ½ a mile, passing Eaglescliffe Golf Club and Teesside High Schoo,l before turning right opposite Trinity Methodist Church. Follow this path

Quarry Wood Nature Reserve

down into a wooded area next to the river and then continue with the river immediately on your right. Enter Quarry Wood Nature Reserve which comprises wooden walk ways and parkland.

Eventually the path turns away from the river to climb well established steps to a tarmac road. Turn right and after 50 yards do not go straight on but bear left under a metal archway of leaves.

After 400 yards emerge onto a dual carriageway and walk left along the pedestrian path to a road island. At the island go right to Bowesfield Park. Follow this road downhill until it runs out and then go right onto a path through Bowesfield Conservation Area. On reaching the river turn left and walk with the river (which is now much wider) on your right. After a mile walk under the A66 by passing under three bridges and then turn away from the river up a tarmac road to meet another road. Turn right and after 400 yards cross the A3015 and then a car park to the bottom left hand corner by the river. The path then goes round the back of the replica of the *HMS Bark Endeavour* and returns to the river. Walk under a wonderful footbridge and then through a delightful riverside area at Stockton.

Walk under another bridge bearing the roman numerals MCMXC11 and past the Castlegate Marine Club access before passing under another beautiful footbridge. Walk up to the Tees Barrage and through the White Water Centre (there are several routes) and continue on the riverside

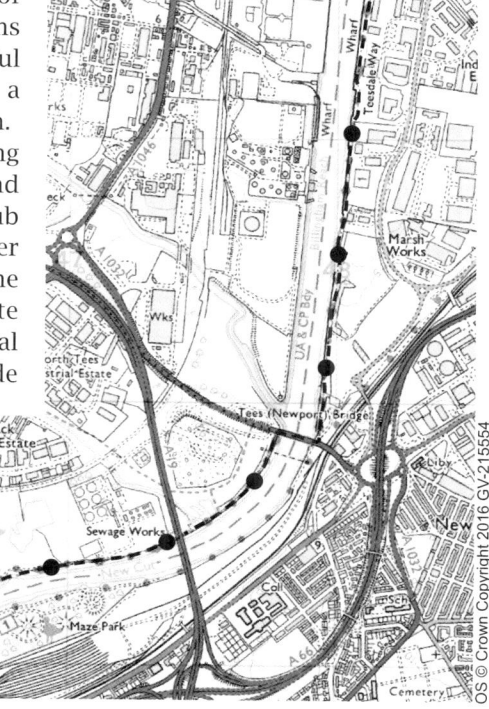

path, through another small nature reserve, to pass under the A19.

On arriving at the green metal Newport Bridge climb the steps on the left and then cross over the bridge to the other side of the river. Once there take great care crossing the road before descending to the riverside path now on the right of the river. After 1.5 miles turn right away from the river and after passing through a park with metallic dinosaurs emerge onto a road. Turn left and walk 0.8 of a mile to the Transporter Bridge.

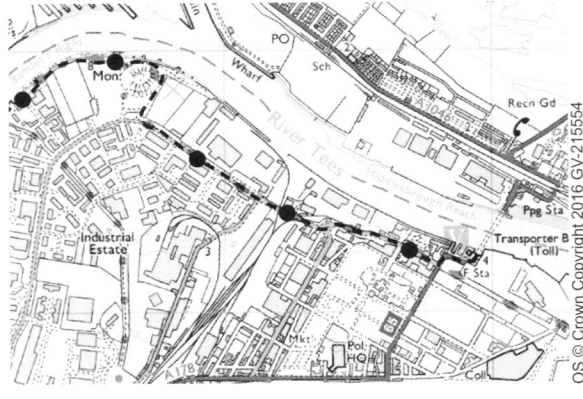

Newport Bridge

The Transporter Bridge at Middlesbrough

BRIAN CLOUGH AT MIDDLESBROUGH

Brian Clough was a prolific goal scorer at his first, and home town, club scoring 204 goals in 222 games.

In 1995, Middlesbrough F.C. moved to the Riverside Stadium from Ayresome Park which had been the home of the club from its construction in time for the 1903-04 season.

The Riverside can be seen from the Transporter Bridge. The original location of Ayresome Park is now a housing estate with roads named after the Middlesbrough F.C. legends.

For those wishing to visit the site
Walk away from the river towards the town up Durham Street, which becomes Cleveland Street. Pass under the A66 and turn right into Wilson Street. With

the A66 immediately on your right, follow this road round as it becomes the wide Newport Road. This is the B6541 and follow it to the next major roundabout. Bear left down the A1032 Hayward Street until you reach Ayresome Street on your left. Turn left and then immediately right into Ayresome Green Lane. Clough Close is the next road on the left. This is where Ayresome Park was originally sited. (Distance 2 miles)

You may also wish to visit the Brian Clough statue in Albert Park and his birthplace close by at 11, Valley Road.

Details can also be obtained of a walk from Don Revie's birthplace to Valley Road.

Brian Clough statue in Albert Park

MIDDLESBROUGH TO HARTLEPOOL
10.3 miles

Use the Transporter Bridge (a small toll has to be paid) to cross the river and then follow the road round underneath the railway and past the Station Hotel. Walk up the A1046 passing the Clarence Kickwall recreation area on your right and after a mile the road turns sharp left to a set of traffic lights. Go right up Hope Street and walk up this road for 1.3 miles taking great care to face any oncoming traffic. Arrive at the lovely little village of Cowpen Bewley and walk up to the junction. Walk left for 100 yards and then opposite the Three Horse Shoes pub go right up Wolverston Pack Lane and over a level crossing. After 200 yards turn right up a lane sign posted to Cowpen Bewley Woodland Park.

Greatham

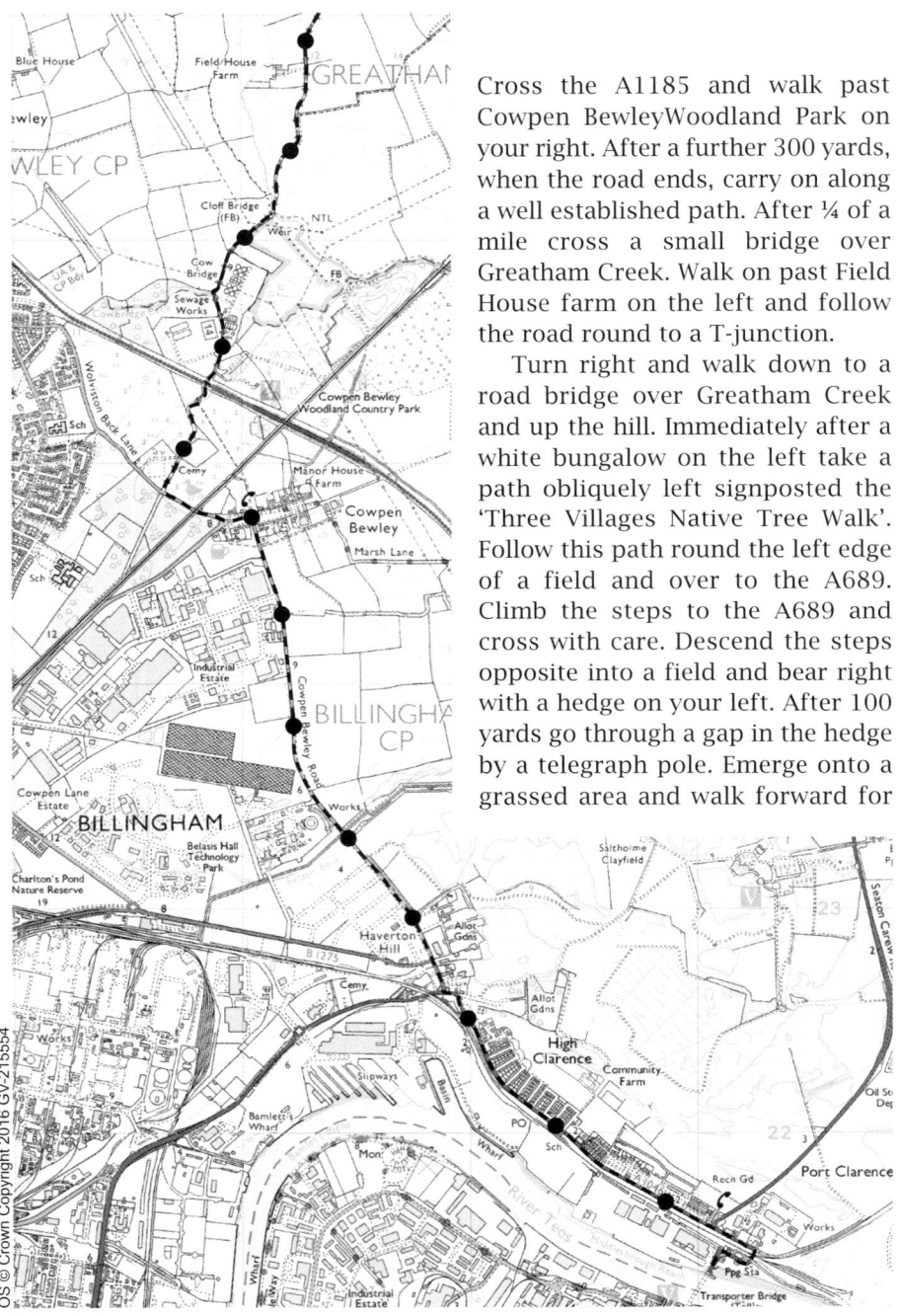

Cross the A1185 and walk past Cowpen BewleyWoodland Park on your right. After a further 300 yards, when the road ends, carry on along a well established path. After ¼ of a mile cross a small bridge over Greatham Creek. Walk on past Field House farm on the left and follow the road round to a T-junction.

Turn right and walk down to a road bridge over Greatham Creek and up the hill. Immediately after a white bungalow on the left take a path obliquely left signposted the 'Three Villages Native Tree Walk'. Follow this path round the left edge of a field and over to the A689. Climb the steps to the A689 and cross with care. Descend the steps opposite into a field and bear right with a hedge on your left. After 100 yards go through a gap in the hedge by a telegraph pole. Emerge onto a grassed area and walk forward for

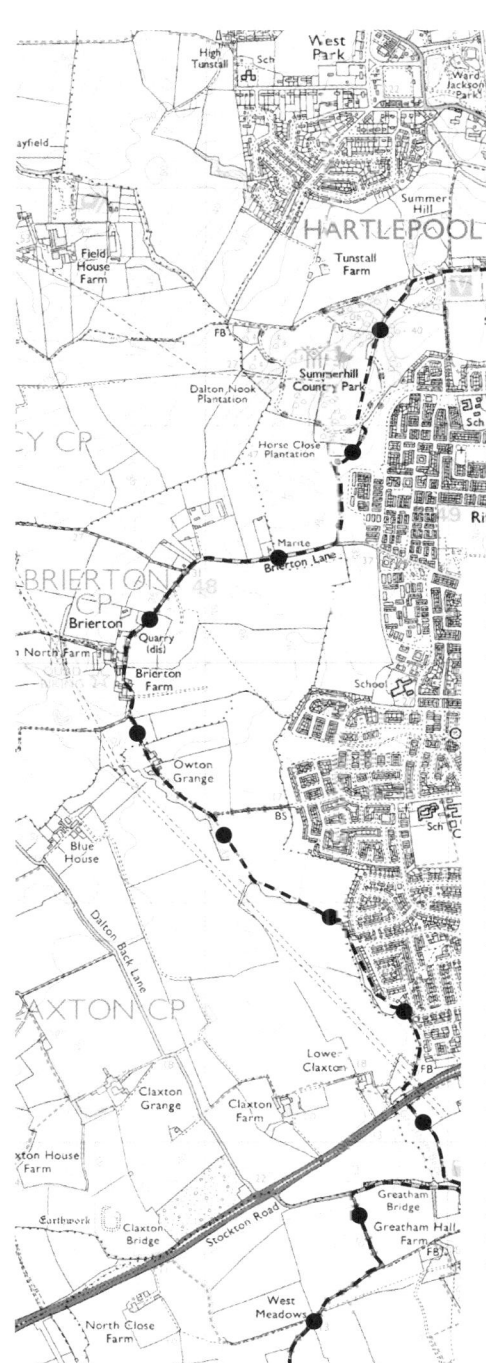

with houses on your right and the beck on your left for 0.4 of a mile. When the path next to the houses turns right go left through a metal kissing gate to remain next to the beck. Walk next to the beck and on the left of two fields until you meet a farm road. Turn left and walk along the road to Brierton Farm. The path passes to the left of the farm house between outbuildings. 300 yards past the farm pass through a farm gate on to a road and turn right up the hill. Walk between more farm buildings and continue along Brierton Lane. After 0.3 of a mile enter a path on the left accessed via an old cattle grid and metal squeeze-through stile. Walk along a tree lined path to emerge into a wide grassed area with houses to the right. At the end of the grassed area go through a gate on the left into Summer Hill Country Park and turn right to walk through the park, past a playground and round to the Visitor Centre.

Walk past the Visitor Centre, over a roundabout and down Summer Hill road to a T-junction. Cross the road, walk a few yards to the left and enter Family Wood. After 100 yards turn right into Burn Valley Gardens. Now simply follow the burn through the gardens. After ¼ of a mile cross a road and continue through the gardens until they terminate at a roundabout on York Road. Go left up York Road for ½ a mile and turn right into Victoria Road. Walk to the war memorial on the right.

Summerhill Country Park Visitor Centre

Hartlepool War Memorial

BRIAN CLOUGH AT HARTLEPOOL

Hartlepool United Football Club

Brian Clough's first managerial position was from 1965 to 1967, the youngest manager in the Football League at 30 years old. Hartlepool had applied for re-election to the league in five of the previous seasons before Brian arrived. Financially the club was in dire straits. Brian had to badger local pubs to raise funds and aquire a coach driver licence to drive the team bus. The season before he left they finished 8th in the league.

The walk goes right past the ground.

HARTLEPOOL TO SEAHAM
14 miles

From the war memorial cross the road and walk right past the civic centre. Take Swainson Road on the left and after 100 yards turn right down Museum Street. At the end of Museum Street turn left at the roundabout up Clarence Road and walk past the *HMS Trincomalee* on your right and the Hartlepool United Victoria Park football ground on your left. Go straight across the traffic lights into Lancaster Road. At the T-junction at the top turn right into Powlett Road, walk under a bridge and bear left onto the continuation of Lancaster Road. Almost immediately take a path on the left through a housing estate, to the right of the Phoenix Centre and on a further 200 yards to West View Road the A1049. Cross the road, go left and then immediately right up a cycle track. After 100 yards the path bears left up to a disused road. Cross the road

The beach at Hartlepool

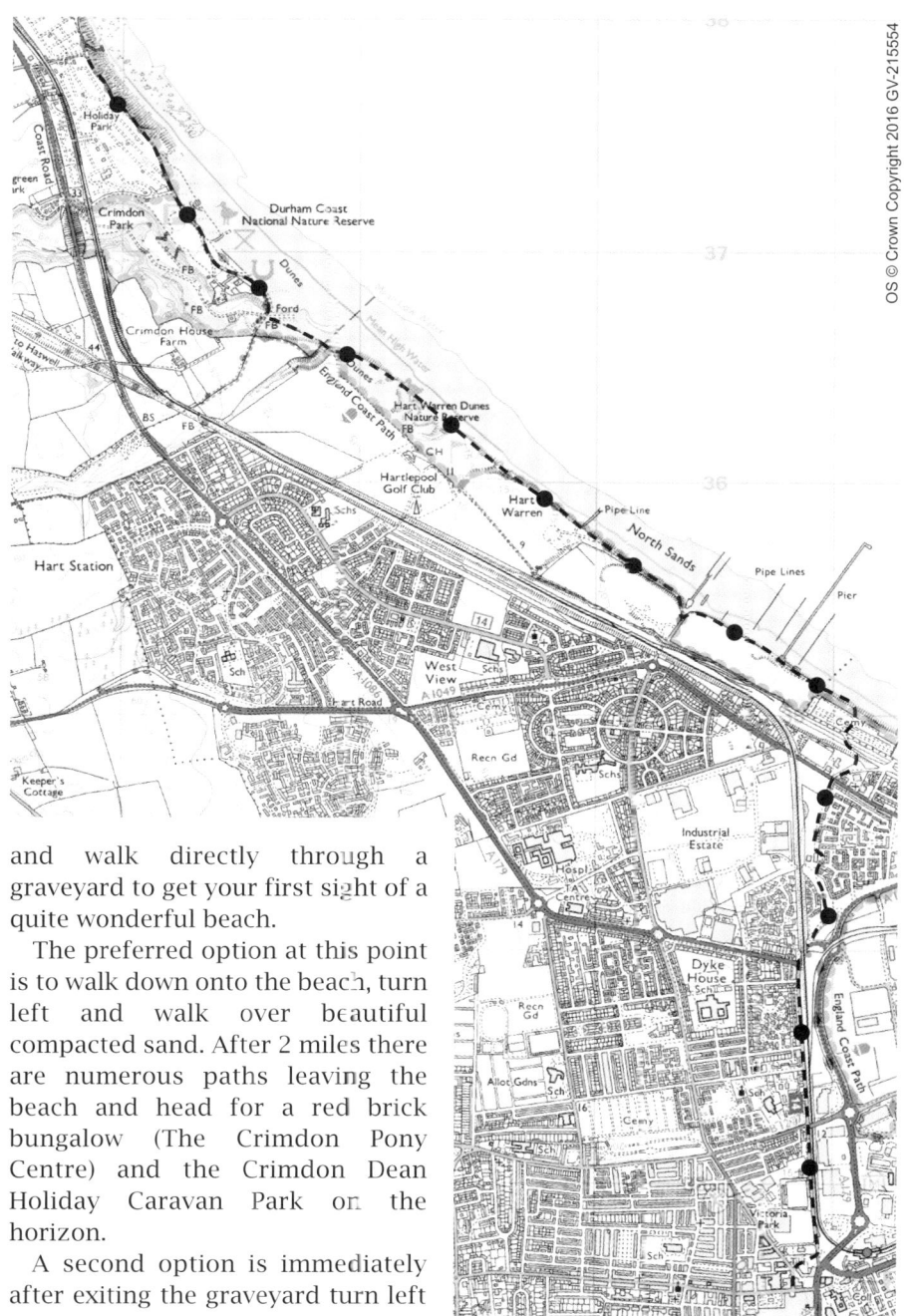

and walk directly through a graveyard to get your first sight of a quite wonderful beach.

The preferred option at this point is to walk down onto the beach, turn left and walk over beautiful compacted sand. After 2 miles there are numerous paths leaving the beach and head for a red brick bungalow (The Crimdon Pony Centre) and the Crimdon Dean Holiday Caravan Park on the horizon.

A second option is immediately after exiting the graveyard turn left

Looking towards Crimdon Dean

and follow a path adjacent to the beach, above the sand dunes, past Hartlepool Golf Club, and up to Crimdon Dean.

Whichever route you choose, the caravans at Crimdon Dean are clearly visible and your destination never in doubt.

From the parking area and road at Crimdon Dean follow the path through the Crimdon Dean Holiday Park to the open grassed area at the other end. Make for the bottom left hand corner of the grassed area next to the railway bridge. Do not pass under the bridge but continue right with the railway line on your left and pass an area fenced off with metal fencing on your right. After 300 yards the path goes down steps into a gill and up the other side. Go over a stile and turn right towards the coast. After 100 yards cross over two double stiles and then turn left along the top of the cliffs. After 300 yards do not take the path left to the Blackhall Rocks car park but continue forward on the coastal path. After a further 100 yards descend into a gill and up the steps on the other side. On arriving at a small car park, cross the road and continue on the path via a metal gate. This is a stoney path with grass down

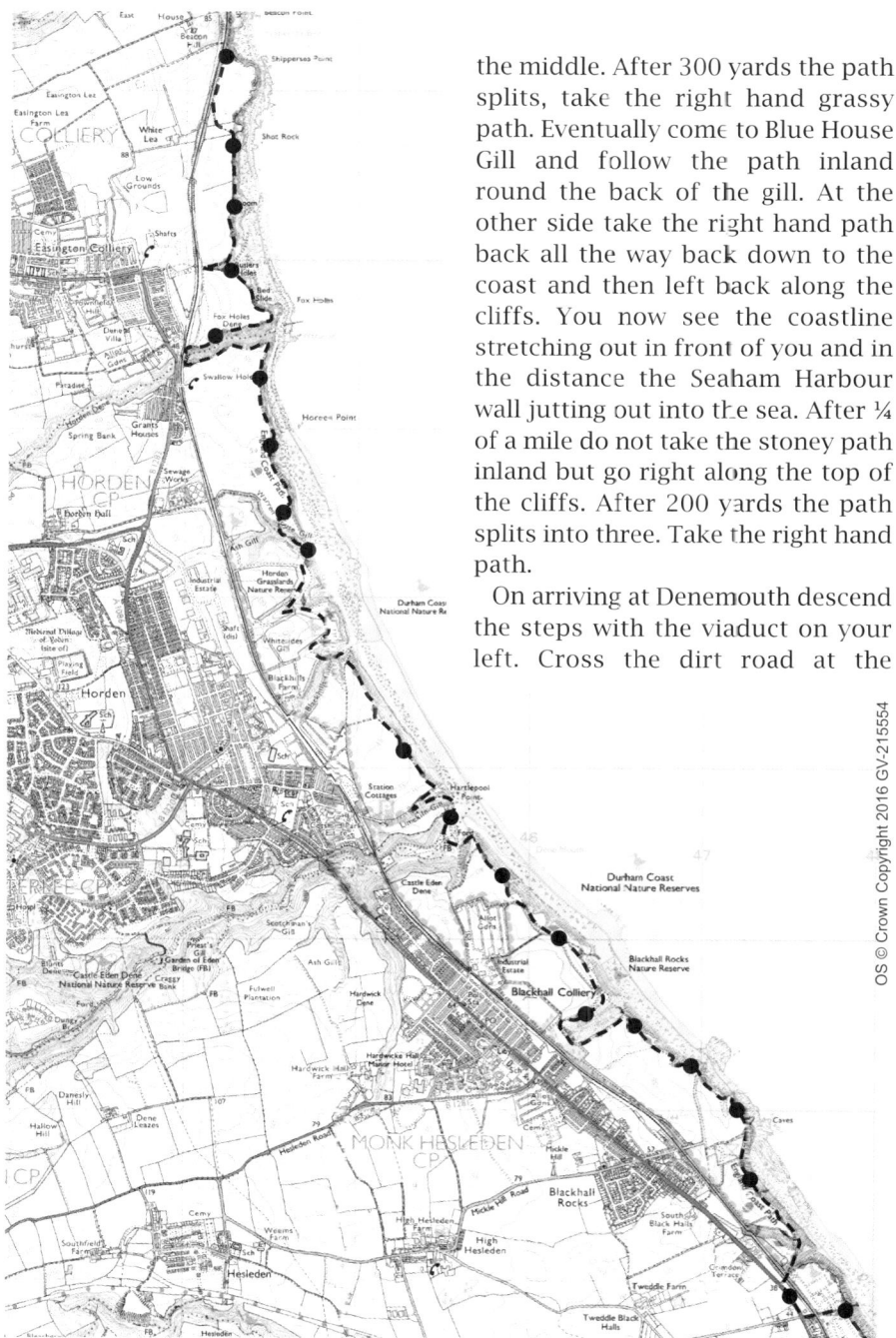

the middle. After 300 yards the path splits, take the right hand grassy path. Eventually come to Blue House Gill and follow the path inland round the back of the gill. At the other side take the right hand path back all the way back down to the coast and then left back along the cliffs. You now see the coastline stretching out in front of you and in the distance the Seaham Harbour wall jutting out into the sea. After ¼ of a mile do not take the stoney path inland but go right along the top of the cliffs. After 200 yards the path splits into three. Take the right hand path.

On arriving at Denemouth descend the steps with the viaduct on your left. Cross the dirt road at the bottom and continue on the path towards the bridge with green metal railings. On the other side of the bridge don't take the path towards the viaduct but walk towards the sea and round the headland. Now walk up the road away from the sea, pass through a car park and, after a further 100 yards, turn right between big wooden posts onto a stoney path towards the sea.

On bearing left along the cliffs pass a metal bird sculpture on your left. On arriving at Blackhills Gill follow the steps down to the bottom of the gill. On meeting a grassed path turn left and walk up the gill away from the sea. At the top of the gill bear right up a well laid stone path next to a concrete water channel. At the top turn right across the concrete channel and on meeting a grass path turn right back towards the sea. The path soon turns inland again around the back of Whitesides Gill. At Warren House Gill do not turn left into the car park but go straight on down the steps. At the bottom of the steps turn left and walk up the gill away from the sea. At the back of the gill go right over a stile and up the wooden steps. At the top continue on the grass path heading north. Cross over a stile on your left that is perilously close to

The Durham coastal path

Looking back to Blackhall Rocks

the cliff edge. On reaching Foxholes Dene follow the path sharply to the left and inland. At the top of the dene walk through woodland and out of the dene to a railway bridge on your left. Turn right towards the coast. After 30 yards bear left onto a stoney path.

At the next railway bridge continue straight ahead with railway line on your left. Across the railway line you will see a parkland area which was the Easington Colliery site. Where the path turns right over a red brick bridge do not follow it but bear right down a bank and skirt a field with the railway immediately on your left. Go through two metal gates with the sea approximately 200 yards to your right. Eventually turn left under Hawthorn Viaduct. Do not take the steep path down to your right but walk up the dene for 30 yards before taking a path right back towards the viaduct. Before reaching the viaduct descend the wooden steps on your left.

At the bottom of the steps turn left past a cave on your left and over a concrete and metal walk bridge. Ascend the steps on the other side with a metal hand rail on your left. Follow the path round and out through a kissing gate. After about 50 yards turn right up to the railway line, cross the stile, the railway line and the stile on the other side.

Turn left with the railway now on your left. At the next bridge continue straight ahead keeping the railway on your left. You should now see Seaham Harbour lighthouse. Pass through a metal gate and to an information board at Noses Point.

Follow the path to the left but then immediately take the right fork over a metal bridge. Turn right and then take any of the grass paths off to the right. Head for the car park with the stone wall on the edge of the cliff. Having walked through the car park follow the well established cliff path to the main harbour road, turn right and take the waymarked promenade path down past the harbour on your right.

At the roundabout continue in a northerly direction straight ahead and pass the war memorial on your right. Leave the shopping area and walk along the promenade to the next roundabout. At the roundabout stay on the

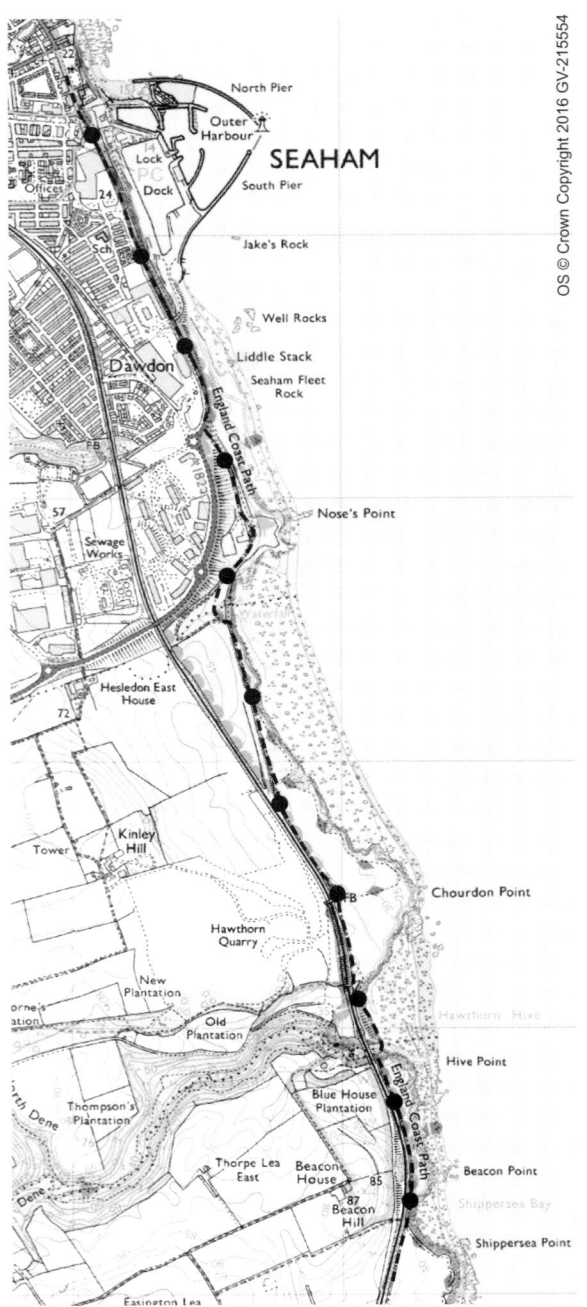

112

pavement on the right and walk straight ahead. On reaching a car park bear right through the car park and go down some steps. Bear right along the pavement and walk up to a second car park. This is the Seaham Hall Beach car park.

Approaching Seaham

SEAHAM TO ROKER PARK
8 miles

Leave the Hall Beach car park at Seaham on the B1287. After half a mile the road turns left under a railway bridge. Do not pass under the bridge but take the public footpath to the right. Do not descend the steps but go down the 24-hour emergency access road. Proceed towards the coast. On reaching a stile do not cross it but bear left along the right hand edge of a field to the cliff top. At the wooden marker post stop to enjoy excellent retrospective views of the Hall Beach, Seaham Harbour and the North Yorkshire coast in the distance.

Now continue north along the cliff path with Sunderland ahead of you. Be sure to keep strictly to the cliff path as the cliffs are liable to erosion. In the past you would have been able to see the floodlights of Roker Park but football has now moved to the Stadium of Light. After half a mile the path

Seaham Hall beach

takes the form of a two wheel vehicle track through grass. At the next inlet the track moves inland towards the railway line. The path eventually goes down to the right to a road in front of a railway bridge. Do not go under the bridge but cross the road to take the track up again on the other side. After a short distance on concrete the path becomes a vehicle track again with the railway on your left. After ¾ of a mile do not turn left under the railway line but continue on the track as it bears to the right.

Pass a new road bridge on your left but do not cross it. After ¼ of a mile take a track right which brings you onto another track next to the coast. Proceed in a northerly direction. Follow the track down to the sea front at Hendon. It was at this point that we asked a local man walking his dog for directions to the River Wear. He replied "Yu just keep gannin til yu canna gan nee forther".

The beech at Hendon

Continue along the sea front with the railings on your right. At the storage tanks at the end turn left up the road which then turns right and then left under the railway line. Follow this road up to the main road and then turn right. Walk towards a roundabout with the Raich Carter (another great

Sunderland football hero) Sports Centre on your left. At the roundabout continue straight on. At the next roundabout bear right on the B1522 to the Port. Pass the high rise flats named D'arcy Court on your left hand side. At the next roundabout do not take the B1294 to the city centre but carry straight on into a road cordoned off with concrete bollards. Walk past Hope church on the left. At the roundabout go straight on down Donnison Gardens and into Greys Cross.

The Town Bridge Sunderland

At the bottom of Walton Lane cross the road and walk down to Keyside House. Turn left and walk up the cobbled lane with the river Wear on your right. Continue in the same direction along Low Street. At the top of the hill turn right and cross the Town Bridge. You can now see the new Sunderland A.F.C. ground, the Stadium of Light, to your left.

At the other side of the bridge take the steep steps which hug the side of the bridge down to the river. At the bottom of the steps turn left and walk along the riverside with the bridge now behind you. Walk past the Sunderland University Library on your left. After passing the Throwing Stone Cafe in the

Glass Centre on your right the path moves gradually away from the river, passes houses on your left and arrives at a road. Go left down the road towards the marina. Walk left along the back of the marina and through a car park, exiting it at the top left corner into a road. At the top of the road go left and then right and walk down to the harbour. At a mini-roundabout turn left and walk left along the sea front to the end of the promenade. At the end of the promenade walk down onto the sand. This is the official end of the walk. The entrance to Roker Park is through two bridges on your left. (Not the old football ground but an actual park!)

The end! Roker beach with the entrance to Roker Park on your left. Why not relax on the beautiful beach. You've earned it.

BRIAN CLOUGH AT SUNDERLAND

His second and last club as a player scoring 63 goals in 74 matches.

Sunderland A.F.C. moved from Roker Park to the Stadium of Light in 1997. The new stadium can be seen from the walk when crossing the Wear Bridge.

If you wish to visit the site of the old football ground then fork right at the band stand. Walk past a bowling green on your right and do not exit the park but take the path on the left. Walk past a second bowling green and a boating lake and after passing toilets on your left exit the park onto a road. Turn right and walk towards the New Derby Public House. Pass Ashdale Court on your right and on reaching Grantham Road you are now looking at the site of the old Roker Park Stadium. This definitely is the end of your walk.

A picture of Roker Park displayed in The Stadium of Light

MILEAGE CHARTS

Trent Bridge to Sawley	10.8
Sawley to Derby	9.6
Derby to Belper	8.5
Belper to Matlock	10.5
Matlock to Baslow	9.2
Baslow to Heatherdene	11
Heatherdene to Langsett	12.5
Langsett to Clayton West	8.5
Clayton West to Batley	14.5
Batley to Apperley Bridge	11.5
Apperley Bridge to Harewood	12.3
Harewood to Knaresborough	9.7
Knaresborough to Boroughbridge	9.4
Borough bridge to Thirsk	11.5
Thirsk to Brompton	12
Brompton to Yarm	13.5
Yarm to Middlesbrough	11.7
Middlesbrough to Hartlepool	10.3
Hartlepool to Seaham	13
Seaham to Roker Park	8
Total	218

LOCATION	DISTANCE TO	TOTAL DISTANCE
Trent Bridge		
Beeston Marina	4.5 miles	4.5 miles
Sawley	5.3 miles	10.8 miles
Borrowash	4.7 miles	15.5 miles
Derby	4.9 miles	20.4 miles
Duffield Bridge	5.0 miles	25.4 miles
Belper	3.5 miles	28.9 miles
Ambergate	2.7 miles	31.6 miles
Cromford	5.1 miles	36.7 miles
Matlock	2.7 miles	39.4 miles
Rowsley	5.0 miles	44.4 miles
Baslow	4.2 miles	48.6 miles
Grindleford	4.0 miles	52.6 miles
Shatton	4.6 miles	57.2 miles
Heatherdene	2.4 miles	59.6 miles
Howden Dam	5.2 miles	64.8 miles
Langsett	7.3 miles	72.1 miles
Thurlston	2.4 miles	74.5 miles
Lower Denby	3.5 miles	78 miles
Clayton West	2.6 miles	80.6 miles
Flockton	3.6 miles	84.2 miles
Thornhill Edge	2.5 miles	86.7 miles
Dewsbury	5.5 miles	92.2 miles
Batley	2.9 miles	95.1 miles
Gildersome	2.7 miles	97.8 miles
Pudsey	4.6 miles	102.4 miles
Apperley Bridge	4.2 miles	106.6 miles
Scotland	4.4 miles	111 miles
Golden Acre Park	3.1 miles	114.1 miles
Harewood	4.8 miles	118.9 miles
Spofforth	5.5 miles	124.4 miles
Knaresborough	4.2 miles	128.6 miles
Arkendale	4.8 miles	133.4 miles

Arkendale	4.8 miles	133.4 miles
Boroughbridge	4.6 miles	138 miles
Dalton	7.3 miles	145.3 miles
Thirsk	4.2 miles	149.5 miles
Thornton le Moore	5.0 miles	154.5 miles
Northallerton	5.0 miles	159.5 miles
Brompton	2.0 miles	161.5 miles
Deighton	4.5 miles	166 miles
Appleton Whiske	2.4 miles	168.4 miles
Yarm	6.6 miles	175 miles
Eaglescliffe	3.0 miles	178 miles
Stockton on Tees	4.0 miles	182 miles
Middlesbrough	4.7 miles	186.7 miles
Greatham	5.4 miles	192.1 miles
Hartlepool	4.9 miles	197 miles
Crimdon Dean	4.0 miles	201 miles
Fox Holes	5.0 miles	206 miles
Seaham	4.0 miles	210 miles
Hendon	4.0 miles	214 miles
Roker	4.0 miles	218 miles

MAPS AND GUIDES

Ordnance Survey Maps 259, 260, OL24, 288, 289, 299, 302, 304, 306, 308 and Ordnance Survey Outdoor Leisure 1.

The Trent Valley Way
The Derwent Valley Heritage Way
The Kirklees Way
The Leeds Country Way
The Three Villages Native Tree Walk
The Teesdale Way
The Durham Coastal Path

TOURIST INFORMATION CENTRE TELEPHONE NUMBERS

Nottingham	0844 477 5678
Derby	01332 643411
Peak District (Bakewell)	
(for Belper, Baslow, Grindleford and Bamford)	01629 816558
Dewsbury	01924 325080
Leeds	01332 425242
Knaresborough	01423 866886
Boroughbridge	01423 323373
Thirsk	01845 522755
Northallerton	01609 776864
Stockton on Tees (for Yarm)	01642 528130
Middlesborough	01642 729900
Hartlepool	01429 869706
Sunderland	0191 5532000

Martin Perry is a retired Deputy Head, schools football coach, a published author and latterly a professional musician. He was born in Cheshire but when his parents moved to Sunderland in 1967 became a lifelong Sunderland AFC fan.

He is married to Chris and moved from Sunderland to live and work in Nottingham in 1969.

He is a keen walker and has walked most of the established long distance trails with Geoff.

Geoff is also a retired Deputy Head, classical musician and avid sports fan. Geoff was born in Nottingham and has lived there all his life. He is a Nottingham Forest fan and also has a passion for long distance walking.

Also from Sigma Leisure:

Heart of England Way
102 miles of linear walk or 225 miles of 32 linked circular walks
Stephen J Cross

A book both for the long distance and the leisure walker, The Heart of England Way, and 32 circular walks, takes the walker on a journey slicing through the quieter areas of midland, shire, countryside; from the north edge of Cannock Chase, to Bourton on the Water; providing a fascinating view through the back door of the regions history, people, buildings and landscape.
£8.99

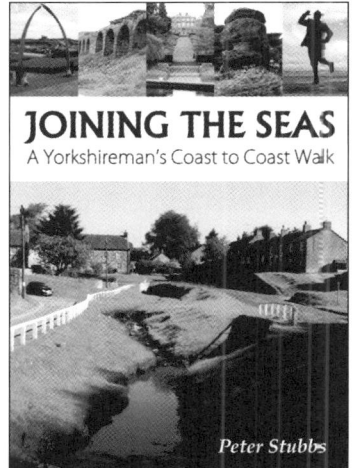

Joining the Seas
A Yorkshireman's Coast to Coast Walk
Doug Brown

An alternative to Wainwright's iconic Coast-to-Coast walk, this 150-mile trek across northern England focuses on some of the historic towns and villages, ruined abbeys and stunning landscape features of Yorkshire, voted third in the list of top 10 world regions to visit in Lonely Planet's Best in Travel guide for 2014. Beginning at Whitby the walk traverses the North York Moors, the Vale of York, the Nidderdale Area of Outstanding Natural Beauty, the Yorkshire Dales and the northern edge of the Forest of Bowland, before finishing with a short hop through Lancashire at its narrowest point to reach Morecambe on the West coast. The walk has been divided into seventeen stages, varying in length from less than four to around 15 miles that can be combined to suit individual tastes.
£8.99

River Tyne Trail: from source to sea
Donaghy & Laidler

The trail traces the length of one of Britain's greatest rivers, the Tyne. The 130 mile walk covers both sources, the North and South Tynes, which are marked by giant stone monuments. From tiny springs to streams and then vibrant rivers, the two sources eventually converge to create the powerful River Tyne as it journeys to the sea. The nature of the undulating terrain makes for a challenging and rewarding experience as the trail passes through some of Britain's most beautiful and interesting scenery. This book is the brainchild of former businessman Brian Burnie, the founder of the Cancer Patient Care Charity 'Daft as a Brush'. Brian hopes that this walk will promote the work of the charity which provides individualised transport for patients requiring cancer treatment.

£12.99

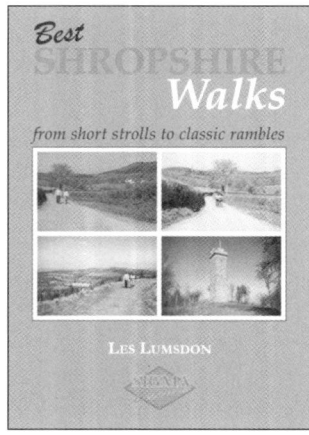

Best Shropshire Walks 2nd Ed
from short strolls to classic rambles
Les Lumsdon

A new revised edition of this much loved guide contains 36 walks, located in all parts of the county. Several walks feature fine hill walking on the Welsh borders and others start from delightful villages and hamlets in the north and east of the county. The Shropshire countryside really comes alive in this well-researched book. All of the walks include stories about the locality: folklore and legends, attractions and facilities. There are clear maps and a selection of photographs to make for an enjoyable and informative read.

£8.99

All of our books are available through booksellers. For a free catalogue, please contact:

Sigma Leisure, Stobart House, Pontyclerc, Penybanc Road, Ammanford SA18 3HP. Tel: 01269 593100 Fax: 01269 596116

info@sigmapress.co.uk   www.sigmapress.co.uk